Tiago do Carmo Nogueira

Blind and sighted users' experience of responsive web design

Tiago do Carmo Nogueira

Blind and sighted users' experience of responsive web design

A comparative study

ScienciaScripts

Imprint
Any brand names and product names mentioned in this book are subject to trademark, brand or patent protection and are trademarks or registered trademarks of their respective holders. The use of brand names, product names, common names, trade names, product descriptions etc. even without a particular marking in this work is in no way to be construed to mean that such names may be regarded as unrestricted in respect of trademark and brand protection legislation and could thus be used by anyone.

Cover image: www.ingimage.com

This book is a translation from the original published under ISBN 978-3-330-76786-7.

Publisher:
Sciencia Scripts
is a trademark of
Dodo Books Indian Ocean Ltd. and OmniScriptum S.R.L publishing group

120 High Road, East Finchley, London, N2 9ED, United Kingdom
Str. Armeneasca 28/1, office 1, Chisinau MD-2012, Republic of Moldova, Europe
Managing Directors: Ieva Konstantinova, Victoria Ursu
info@omniscriptum.com

Printed at: see last page
ISBN: 978-620-8-57536-6

Summary

Access to information on the Web is still a challenge for the community of people with some kind of visual impairment. Research reports that just applying accessibility guidelines to web content is insufficient, thus necessitating a more thorough investigation into the user experience of accessible applications. With the emergence of new design trends on the Web, including responsive design and flat design, it is imperative to investigate the impact of these new ways of transmitting information on the Web. This study aims to identify, classify and compare the differences and similarities in the user experience of Responsive Design with flat and minimalist elements, considering blind and sighted users, correlating emotional impact, usability and performance. A case study was therefore carried out, adopting an exploratory approach, using the *Affect Grid* and *PANAS* methods. Data was extracted using Usability and UX questionnaires. Qualitative and quantitative indicators were used in the analyses to help understand pragmatic UX phenomena. The results show that for blind users, the average inconvenience in responsive websites increases by 20% (twenty per cent) when compared to non-responsive users. For sighted users, the average scores for irritation, embarrassment, determination and dynamism were higher on responsive websites than on non-responsive websites. Thus, responsive websites had a significantly higher median task completion time than non-responsive ones. It can be concluded that in all the subgroups that were compared using this approach, blind users had a significantly lower mean value on the enjoyment scale on responsive websites when compared to sighted users, making the UX of blind people worse on responsive websites when compared to non-responsive ones.

Key words

Accessibility, Usability, User Experience

Summary

CHAPTER 1

Introduction

The Internet was originally conceived for scientific purposes, but it has become a new way of communicating, reaching a large part of the world's population [90]. The growing demand for resources made available by the Web has increased in recent years, as has scientific interest in investigating or promoting the construction of more accessible websites. In this way, part of the user population with some kind of visual impairment, for example blind users, can navigate websites with the help of assistive tools.

At the beginning of this decade, the US census indicated that one in eight American citizens would have some kind of serious disability [90]. In Brazil, around 14.5 per cent of the population has some kind of visual impairment, approximately 27 million people [44]. Some studies report that, in the United States, 10 million people with some kind of disability represent a market estimated at 46 billion dollars. This significant number of people cannot be disregarded when it comes to computer technologies.

Even so, at a time when we are debating the Web as a human right, access to this information is a challenge for the community of users with some kind of visual impairment. Research reports that the application of the Web Content *Accessibility Guidelines* (WCAG*)* alone is insufficient due to factors that are often overlooked by web development professionals [33]. It can be seen that the interaction problems encountered by visually impaired users in the web environment are mainly triggered by poorly designed websites.

Some of the accessibility issues are not identified with the application of WCAG, requiring a new approach to solve problems that go beyond the simple application of accessibility guidelines [45]. To reduce the impact of these problems, measuring the experience of blind users on websites is one of the approaches that can be used to investigate the accessibility and usability of these websites.

In recent years, with the emergence of new trends on the web, such as Responsive Design, new challenges have arisen in the field of research to understand the impact
of this new trend in interactions with users. Responsive Design is a new way of making the website adaptive to the context, i.e. the *layout* adapts according to the user's screen resolution [54]. This new design style has become commonplace in recent years in web interface construction.

1.1 Problem and Justification

Websites are fundamental tools for communication, disseminating information and providing services, especially for people with visual impairments. The web is an essential factor for social and occupational integration for people with special needs.

However, for millions of people around the world, interacting with websites is a challenging task. This is due to poor usability and poor user experience (UX) on websites.

In this sense, websites that have a poor user experience leave visually impaired and blind people at a disadvantage in the information society, where online tasks are becoming more frequent. Thus, the inability to access the Web can have serious socio-economic implications, including increased unemployment and growing dependence on governments to provide funding for this segment of the world's population [15].

Undoubtedly, the Web is far from fulfilling its potential to serve all users. Inaccessible and unusable sites abound. Even sites that are theoretically accessible often have poor usability for people with disabilities. Lack of usability and a poor user experience mean that tasks on websites become difficult to carry out, resulting in poor performance among users during interactions.

According to Nielsen (2007), **sighted** users perform tasks in Web interfaces 3 (three) times faster than blind users, when it is possible for them to perform the tasks themselves [68]. Bigham (2007) presented a more recent study, on selected tasks, in which blind users took 4.5 (four point five) times longer than sighted users to perform the tasks [8].

In turn, website design has undergone radical changes in terms of design, development and construction in recent years [71]. Today, therefore, there are several aspects that need to be adopted when it comes to Web Design [71], for example Responsive Design for mobile devices, interactivity and *Fiat Design.* In this sense, these transformations can be seen as new trends applied to the design and construction of web pages.

Thus, in order to measure the emotional aspects during interactions in responsive design with minimalist elements, there is a need to carry out careful research into the experience of blind and sighted users when using these new web trends. Thus, the following question arises: What are the differences and similarities in the user experience of new web trends between blind and sighted users, considering emotional and efficiency aspects?

1.2 Research Relevance

The relevance of carrying out studies on user experience, going beyond usability and accessibility, is due to the fact that UX has become an established field of research [77], with various applications. An example of this applicability can be seen in the design phase of the software development process for *mobile* systems (Lean UX). UX involves a person's emotions about using a particular computing platform, and is subjective in nature, as it is a matter of individual perception and thinking in relation to the platform.

In addition, UX is dynamic, as it is constantly changing over time due to the evolution of circumstances and the emergence of innovations, making it appropriate for evaluating new trends on the Web. UX is a process that changes over time and involves two important qualities: traditional usability in human-computer interaction and accessibility balanced with hedonic and affective design.

1.3 Research Objectives

The main objective of this work is to identify and classify the differences and similarities in user experience in Responsive Design with flat and minimalist elements, considering blind and sighted users, correlating emotional impact, usability and performance. In order to achieve the main objective, the following specific objectives were developed:

- Measuring the emotional impact on the experience of blind and sighted users when interacting with responsive and non-responsive websites;
- To identify the main barriers in the experience of blind and partially sighted users when interacting with responsive and non-responsive websites;
- To compare the performance of blind and sighted users in their interactions with responsive and non-responsive websites;

- To demonstrate the differences and similarities in the experience of blind and sighted users when interacting with responsive and non-responsive websites.

1.4 Methodological Procedures

This research is characterised as a case study, with the aim of evaluating the subjective attributes of UX, adopting an exploratory approach with different methods, using qualitative and quantitative indicators that help to understand the pragmatic phenomena of UX.

According to Maule (2012), the exploratory approach aids user research by investigating the context in which predetermined tasks are carried out, thus helping to understand the habits, motivations and behaviours of different types of users [55].

To carry out this case study, six websites were selected in three categories, and six tasks were carried out on each website to identify and measure the user experience during interactions using the *Affect Grid, PANAS* and Usability questionnaires.

The Chi-Square test was used to analyse the nominal variables in the Usability questionnaires, while the Mann-Whitney and Kruskal-Wallis tests were used for the ordinal variables.

Task completion times were analysed using Kaplan-Meier curves and comparisons were made using the Log Rank Test.

The emotional impact was extracted by analysing the *Affect Grid* and *PANAS* questionnaires. The Chi-Square Test and Fisher's Exact Test were used to check whether the frequency found in a sample deviates significantly from the expected frequency. Spearman's correlations were used for the correlations between performance, emotional impact and Usability.

1.5 Work Organisation

In addition to this chapter, which presents the definition of the problem and the justification, the relevance of the research, the objectives and the methodological procedures, this work is organised as follows:

- In order to lay the foundations for this research, **Chapter 2** provides a theoretical framework with the concepts of web accessibility, web usability, new web design trends and User Experience (UX).

- To ensure the originality and relevance of this research, **Chapter 3** presents a systematic review of the literature on user experience (UX) in the new design trends on the Web, considering a comparison between visually impaired, blind and sighted users, focusing on scientific articles published in the last five years, from January 2009 to January 2015.
- In order to achieve the objectives of this research, **Chapter 4** presents a case study on the user experience of new trends on the Web, proposing an analysis between blind and sighted users in responsive and non-responsive design.
- **Chapter 5** presents and discusses the results of the analyses of the case study proposed in **Chapter 4.**
- **Chapter 6** contains the final conclusions of this work and suggestions for future work.

CHAPTER 2

Theoretical Framework

This chapter presents the theoretical framework on Web Accessibility, Web Usability, new trends on the Web and User Experience.

Section 2.1 presents the concept of web accessibility and the applicable accessibility legislation, accessibility guidelines and how to evaluate them. Section 2.2 presents the concept of usability on the Web and usability evaluation methods.

Section 2.3 will present comparisons between the design styles *Skeu- morphism* and *Fiat Design,* a brief explanation of Responsive Design and User Experience (UX).

2.1 Web accessibility

The term accessibility has gained a lot of prominence on the current national scene, given that guaranteeing access to people with special needs in all social institutions has gained momentum, with the issue of inclusion constantly being debated and brought into focus.

And in the world of the Internet, it couldn't be any different, since this communication and information mechanism aims to promote access for all citizens. Hence the need to propose elements that boost this practice and allow everyone to enjoy the benefits of information and communication technology.

Accessibility on the web, therefore, is not just restricted to instruments used in virtual environments and with the presence of technology, but also requires knowledge in other areas that serve as support for the development of projects and technological practices that, in turn, allow virtual activities to run smoothly and, as a result, the web to be used more dynamically and with a social function.

In this sense, it is important to know more specifically the concept of accessibility, as well as the legislation that guides this social practice. It is also essential to identify the guidelines that govern accessibility, both nationally and internationally, establishing a parallel between them as you get to know their characteristics. Through this knowledge, it is possible to understand how web accessibility evaluations and analysis tools are carried out, given that their guidelines must be respected in order to enable full user access.

1.1.1 Concept of Accessibility

The definition of Accessibility has always been closely linked to the concept of Mobility, because when this social movement began, it was more about promoting access for people who had some kind of physical disability themselves, such as wheelchair users who needed access ramps to enter buildings and move around on pavements and public roads. However, with the evolution of the concepts of the word "disability" itself, this theme has been broadened and, as a result, the universe of people with special needs has become much larger than previously identified [64].

Accessibility therefore creates new possibilities that allow people with special needs to make better use of urban spaces, furniture, transport, information and communication technology in a safe and autonomous way, respecting the peculiarities of each human being and realising that diversity must be valued and consequently taken into account when drawing up development plans [12]. In this way, the concept of access comes closer to how projects should be drawn up so that everyone with a disability or reduced mobility can be reached, given that they have different specificities and characteristics that define them as citizens.

In this sense, as the very concept of accessibility has undergone improvements as society has evolved, there has also been a need for it to be included in the virtual universe. Web accessibility is the realisation of an ideal, since everyone, regardless of their limitations, could enjoy its benefits equally, based on their own adaptations, whether through software or hardware that would make this possible [12].

And as the market and technology itself evolve, especially with regard to mobile devices, which are becoming more and more sophisticated, web content would be available to everyone, at any time or in any space that the user deemed necessary. Even for those who are physically challenged or don't have the right ergonomics, there are also mechanisms that can bring greater comfort and enable more appropriate access so as not to jeopardise their limitations in any way.

Accessibility on the Web, therefore, is not only represented by mechanisms that make it possible to enlarge the font to make it easier to read or the audio option, but also by elements called "assistive technology" that aim to allow access to everyone, given that they mean programmes and physical tools helping the blind (with the insertion of Braille and audio on websites), the deaf, people with reduced mobility, in short, a universe of individuals who previously did not have such instruments to enable them to access the Web [12].

1.1.2 Accessibility legislation

Accessibility legislation has always been more closely linked to the concept of a person with a physical disability, but as society has evolved and citizens have recognised themselves as people with rights, there has consequently been a need to draw up laws that cater for this entire target group.

Various pieces of legislation have emerged in an attempt to promote access for people with special needs in all walks of life; around fifty pieces of legislation, including laws, decrees and ordinances, have sought to provide such accessibility.

However, it is worth highlighting here only the main laws that have been of paramount importance to this universe of individuals, as there were some determinations that did not have much effect for the entire target audience, but only for some specific disabled people, as was the case with the first law that was aimed at them, Law No. 4.169 of December 1962, which formalised the use of Braille for reading and writing for the blind [13], or Law 7.405 of November 1985, which made it compulsory to place the international symbol for access in all places that were suitable for use by people with special needs [13].

The first law that effectively aimed to guarantee the rights of people with disabilities came about in the 1980s, with Law No. 7,853/89, which, among other things, established support for people with disabilities and CORDE (National Coordination for the Integration of People with Disabilities), their social integration, as well as establishing the judicial protection of collective or diffuse interests of these people, and also disciplined and regulated the actions of the Public Prosecutor's Office with regard to the definition of crimes [13].

Law 7.In fact, Law No. 7,853/89 gave the government a series of responsibilities, including in the areas of Education, with the adoption of an educational system aimed at Special Education; in Health, with the establishment of preventive actions, such as family planning, accident prevention, among others; in professional training and job opportunities for these individuals; in Human Resources with investments in training, especially for teachers and education professionals, in order to prepare them to work with students with special needs, thus strengthening Special Education; in Buildings, by making it compulsory to adopt standards aimed at making buildings suitable for disabled people and guaranteeing them access to buildings, means of transport and public places, such as public roads; in the context of the work of the Public Prosecutor's Office, this law also instituted the criminalisation of prejudice, making it a crime punishable by imprisonment of one to four years and payment of a fine [13].

This legislation has brought countless benefits to people with disabilities, not just physical ones, but also cognitive and mental ones, as education has become accessible to all of them and has made it possible to guarantee the fundamental rights of these individuals by making them more involved in society, also through health, education and training, as well as mobility, transport and other rights.

However, the most significant development in terms of accessibility came with Decree No. 5.296 of 2004, which greatly expanded the concept of people with disabilities. Article 5°, paragraph I° of this decree makes it very clear that people with physical, hearing, visual and mental disabilities, and even those with reduced mobility, do not fall into the category of "disabled" per se [12].

This decree came about to solve certain problems related to access in the area of telecommunications and technology, which until then had not been possible for the disabled, given that they did not have the tools to contribute to such access. In this sense, changes were made in the area of fixed and mobile telephony, especially for users with hearing and visual impairments [12]. Thus, as social transformations have taken place, we can also see this metamorphosis in the Accessibility universe, as occurred from the first legislation in the 1960s to 2004.

The biggest development that Decree No. 5.296/04 brought to the national scene was the expansion of accessibility not only to physical and urban environments, but also encompassed the need to adapt the Web for people with disabilities. In its Chapter VI on Access to Information and Communication, more precisely in Art. 27, it determines that government websites must have elements that make it possible for visually impaired people to access information [12],

1.1.3 Web Accessibility Guidelines

In order to meet all the needs of users with disabilities, web accessibility must follow certain parameters that guide this initiative so that all individuals in this universe are fully and equally served.

When it comes to people with special needs, it's interesting to note that the guidelines consider the visually impaired to be blind, colour blind or people with low vision; the hearing impaired to be those individuals who are unable to follow videos and/or audio; and the motorically impaired to be those who have difficulty or no ability to use a keyboard or mouse. This means that all these individuals must be considered when developing accessible content.

There are two sets of essential recommendations to consider when producing an accessible web in Brazil: WCAG and eMAG.

The WCAG (*Web Content Accessibility Guidelines) is* an international initiative and consists of a series of recommendations for accessibility in the web environment. It is used primarily by web developers and occasionally by manufacturers of authoring tools and evaluation tools who are looking to improve their accessibility tools [64].

WCAG has two versions, WCAG 1.0 and WCAG 2.0. WCAG 1.0 contains fourteen fundamental principles [5]:

- Promoting equivalent alternatives to auditory and visual content;
- Don't just use colour;
- Use markup and style sheets correctly;
- Clearly indicate the language used;
- Create tables that can be transformed harmoniously;
- Ensure that pages using new technologies are transformed smoothly;
- Ensure user control over temporal changes in content;
- Ensuring direct accessibility in user-integrated interfaces;
- Design the page with device independence in mind;
- Use provisional solutions;
- Use technologies and recommendations;
- Provide background information and guidance;
- Provide clear navigation mechanisms;
- Ensure that documents are clear and simple.

Each of these principles has a level of priority that allows their applicability to be assessed, which will be presented in the next topic.

WCAG 2.0 was based on the first version, but it has 4 principles (perception, comprehension, operation and robustness) which are subdivided, totalling 12 recommendations. While the first version sought more specifically to address the deficiencies themselves, WCAG 2.0 was built in a more dynamic way, with the collaboration of scholars from different countries, and therefore highlighted more issues relating to different web technologies [64].

In Brazil, there is the e-MAG (Electronic Government Accessibility Manual) which, in turn, has 8 principles, also inspired by WCAG 1.0, with the intention of making web content truly accessible, but formatted to cater for the national public.

In order to check that pages comply with the recommendations, there is the Accessibility Seal recommended by e-MAG. This seal has three levels of accessibility known as A, AA and AAA which represent, respectively, compliance with the priority levels established by the WAI *(Web Accessibility Initiative)* [64],

The e-MAG is available in two versions for consultation: the Technical Booklet and the Accessibility Model. The Technical Booklet, as its name implies, is aimed more at professionals in the field, as its content takes a more technical view of the subject, while the Accessibility Model allows laypeople to understand it better, with content on legislation, accessibility, recommendations and further reading [64].

1.1.4 Web Accessibility Evaluation

Web accessibility assessment can be checked using internationally pre-established levels, which have served as a fundamental basis for drawing up national references for the suitability of web pages for full access by everyone, including people with disabilities.

The WAI established the first way of evaluating or verifying the accessibility of pages, in accordance with the WCAG guidelines. In this way, three levels of priority were established: 1, 2 and 3.0 Level 1 corresponds to what must be done, i.e. the items that must be contained on the web in order for it to have the minimum necessary accessibility. Level 2, on the other hand, refers to what it would be advisable to contain on a page in order to bring it closer to the ideal, although these would not be compulsory items without which access would be possible without major difficulties for certain groups. Level 3 comprises the items that would be the closest to the ideal and would therefore ensure that all users have no difficulty accessing the Web [64].

Brazil, for its part, developed the A, AA and AAA guidelines, which are directly related to the WCAG priority levels, as they took them into account when drafting the e-MAG assessment and also when checking the pages. The "A" recommendation is achieved once level "1" has been completely reached, "AA" is fulfilled when levels "1 and 2" have been reached and, finally, the "AAA" recommendation indicates that levels "1, 2 and 3" have been met. As a reference, the e-MAG also recommends that sites that meet the standards should be awarded the accessibility seal.

An example of this application is the DaSilva[1] website, which was the first Accessibility Evaluator in Portuguese and which developed the "A" evaluation system to give websites the label that best qualifies them within the accessibility scenario and, consequently, determines which web pages are most satisfactory for disabled users. This verifier also has other functions such as providing information, offering web accessibility courses and evaluating pages not only using e-MAG, but also using the rules of WCAG 1.0 and WCAG 2.0.

There is also an automatic validation site that allows you to check whether sites comply with the WCAG standards. The Site AccessMonitor [12] from Portugal, developed by the FCT (Foundation for Science and Technology) makes it possible to evaluate pages by URL, Direct Entry or Uploaded Files, allowing both 1.0 and 2.0 WCAG standards to be checked.

1.1.5 Final considerations

Accessibility on the web is fundamental so that everyone, without distinction, can have access to the content on the pages and also have the right not only to access, but also to be more participatory and contribute to the development of actions that enable a gradual evolution of this issue.

In this sense, it is essential to know about accessibility, even outside the web context, in order to gain a deeper understanding of the characteristics of this target audience and how they can be catered for virtually. Laws, guidelines and evaluations also play an important role in ensuring that web content is fully favourable to people with special needs.

---

[1] www.dasilva.org.br

[2]www.acessibilidade.gov.pt/accessmonitor

As well as following all the regulations laid down by WCAG 1.0, 2.0 and e-MAG and being adapted with magnifying glasses to facilitate access for people with low vision and/or screen readers for blind people, as well as being prepared so that it is possible to install hardware that allows access for disabled people who have some difficulty or can't even use a mouse or keyboard, web content must also have good usability. In this way, usability is an objective aimed at building knowledge and transforming knowledge in order to promote more than just access, but also social development to the extent that use becomes something characteristic of certain social groups.

Accessibility is therefore interlinked with usability, given that it allows disabled people to access the tools designed for them to acquire information and/or produce knowledge in a dynamic, independent and creative way.

2.2 Web Usability

Usability is a very broad and at the same time narrow definition, given that it is realised by a very wide audience, while its uses become very specific from the moment that certain audiences start to use its tools via the Web and, therefore, well-defined information sharing groups are automatically created.

Usability, like accessibility, is therefore of significant importance to the web scene and it is therefore interesting that, before mentioning it, we learn more about the concept of the word and how it has been implemented in the current scenario of websites so that they are adapted and contain certain basic guidelines for accessible and, consequently, functional operation.

Next, the main evaluation methods will be listed, which basically consist of determining whether sites are in fact investing in the basic guidelines and adapting to fulfil them successfully, and some methods may even include user testing, in order to make the experience more realistic and confirm the possibility that a given page is really proposing innovative, creative and usable solutions for the target audience, always taking into account the specific use that certain groups will make of their tools.

2.2.1 Concept of Web Usability

The concept of usability on the Web has undergone some transformations over the years and, consequently, as technologies have improved, so has its concept, making its applicability in the practice of the digital universe more understandable.

The first concept (which emerged in the 1980s) of usability had a very clear restriction on ergonomics and the interrelationship between the individual and the programme. In other words, it was seen that usability was achieved from the moment when the user made the least possible effort to use the product itself, i.e. accessing web pages using the tools provided, thus demonstrating efficiency in the use of the programme's tools [7].

In the 1990s, however, new elements were added to this concept and so usability came to represent something more specific and also brought with it the need to cater for the user, not just in terms of developing a website that met the minimum requirements, but also initiatives aimed at the promptness, efficiency and effectiveness of the product, as well as user satisfaction. Something that could be defined not just as something objective and containing all the minimum requirements for acceptability, but with subjective contributions that demonstrated ease of use and thus approval of the product [7].

In the following decade, due to the popularisation of the internet and, consequently, because it was a period in which various political and social transformations took place, especially in the area of accessibility and social inclusion, there was a deepening of studies in this area and, as a result, some concepts were expanded, several were extinguished and many were evolved, bringing with them characteristics of today's modern society, which is becoming increasingly demanding and always expects to be surprised by what is presented to it as a product or service.

These desires have also occurred in the web environment and, as a result, information and communication technology initiatives have gained momentum. With them came the intention to promote easier usability for people with disabilities.

According to Nielsen and Loranger (2007), usability is an element that provides and favours access to the use of the Web for all individuals. Among these individuals are disabled people who, like all users, need an agile environment that guarantees efficiency during use so that some kind of learning occurs through its use, with as few errors as possible so that it provides satisfaction on the part of the user [68].

There are currently a number of guidelines that must be taken into account in order to make a website usable in such a way that it can achieve its objectives and provide good content for all its users. Several authors have developed recommendations that they believe are fundamental for the Web, such as Jacob Nielsen (one of the leading names in this area), Bruce Tognazzini and, here in Brazil, the specialist Cláudia Dias [14].

In Brazil, the E-Government Usability Primer contains a series of elements inspired by these experts and linked to the main usability problems found on the websites of public organisations in the country, which are considered essential for web usability work to be as close to ideal as possible [14].

In this sense, there are seven main guidelines that must be taken into account in order for a website to be usable [14]:

- Navigation and context, which should prioritise understanding how the site works, making it easy to navigate the pages and quickly identify the functional tools;
- The information load, which means that the content should be very clear and succinct on the interface, allowing the objective of the page to be visualised;
- Autonomy should focus on the user using the site as independently as possible;
- Errors also deserve attention, given the need for rapid assistance and support, as well as the ease with which they can be resolved when committed by the user, in order to enable their autonomy;
- The design, in turn, must always favour the citizen, in order to guarantee objective understanding, more clearly indicating navigation items and, consequently, ensuring their ease;
- The wording refers to the text of the website, which must be clear and allow citizens to fully understand it, using the most familiar vocabulary possible;
- Familiarity and consistency refers to the fact that websites are more receptive, demonstrating that everyone can have access to their content, which is why it is important to bring it closer to people's daily lives and relate it to aspects of their daily lives, allowing citizens to familiarise themselves with it immediately.

Nielsen and Loranger (2007) consider the fundamental characteristics of a website's usability to be its simple and objective nature, good presentation, agility, efficiency, in other words, the whole set of elements that result in user acceptance and success for both those who use the service and those who were responsible for developing it [68].

2.2.2 Usability Evaluation Methods

The guidelines mentioned above can and should be evaluated so that users don't feel disadvantaged when using certain sites, needing help or even being unable to use them when accessing them. It is essential that individuals are familiar with the subject matter, as well as the information and services offered by the site, that they know how to navigate the site in a dynamic and comprehensible way, that they really understand the language found there, that it meets and even exceeds their expectations, otherwise the basics of usability would not be applied by the site.

There are countless ways of assessing usability. According to the Usability Primer (2010) [14], they can be subdivided into three main groups: investigation method, inspection method and user testing.

The Research Method has a more specific research profile, given that its main instruments include questionnaires, interviews, field observation, among others. It is usually carried out at the initial stage of the project, perhaps because it is a methodology that prioritises aspects of acceptability and can be carried out with an ideal number of people that allows for better interpretation of the data, so that any errors found to be occurring at an early stage can be resolved without major damage, thus guaranteeing a greater chance of future success [14]. A highlight of this type of evaluation is Field Observation, which allows the verifier to have their own knowledge of the user's relationship with the product, gathering more precise and objective information about the adoption or non-adoption of minimum usability measures; Interviews are also fundamental, as they provide a more specific understanding of how the citizen sees the use of the resources and functions of the page being used; The Questionnaire, in turn, brings numerous benefits, because it allows access to the largest number of people and it is also possible to allow the individuals themselves to fill it out in order to make them feel more at ease in order to expose their opinion in a more private way, avoiding possible embarrassment on the part of the interviewee [14].

These elements of an investigative nature are essential for the development of the study in question, given the characteristic of better data analysis and collection in the sense that there is a greater guarantee of fidelity in the information, since observation gives the researcher a more direct perception of the facilities and difficulties presented by individuals over a period of using a site, allowing a more independent and centred construction to be carried out regarding the acceptability that a given page has presented and, consequently, whether it really presents usability on the Web. The use of questionnaires and/or interviews is also of significant importance and deserves to be emphasised even more as the use of these instruments guarantees greater reliability and more seriousness to the work, being used as the main source of data collection for the researcher and which, combined with well-developed field observation, gives the study a character of respect, providing consistent foundations so that practice is in fact comparable with the theory studied.

The Inspection Method has more of a checking character that can be applied throughout the development of a website, i.e. it has the function of evaluating whether the usability elements have been fully utilised by the website developers and thus verifying whether the objectives of the institution are being met, in a way that takes into account the focus on the profile of its user.

The main characteristic of this method is the use of checklists of usability principles, i.e. all these recommendations are listed in a checklist and the site is observed in order to see how many and which elements are present on it. In addition, several sites and pages can be evaluated in order to determine how many interfaces follow the established standards, what the main difficulties are and the absence of elements, thus promoting a more quantitative study that does not take much account of the opinion of users, but rather whether the site has strictly followed the recommendations proposed so that usability is in fact being adopted [14],

User testing, on the other hand, generally takes place at all stages of the establishment of usability on the site, so that it adopts a more elaborate position and requires greater preparation on the part of the evaluator, in the sense of investing in an experiment that requires a greater dedication of time and organisation in order to achieve the pre-established objectives and guarantee the success of the work.

This evaluation method has four different main types of tests that can be used throughout the development process, taking into account the levels at which websites are developed in terms of usability. There are comparison, validation, exploration and evaluation tests [14].

Exploration testing is generally used in the early stages of project construction, more specifically when defining requirements and constructing the linear design, given that it provides more in-depth knowledge of the public it will serve, better defining their wishes, desires and expectations regarding the use of the product, thus enabling a well-specified exchange with the client, in this case the user and the evaluator, since this relationship will better define which characteristics should be prioritised for the best usability of the site [14].

Evaluation, on the other hand, is preferably carried out in the middle of development, as it is already possible to check part of the project's progress in order to establish whether the objectives have been met so far and whether it will be possible to adopt all the requirements for implementing usability. The objectives include verifying the execution of real activities and identifying well-defined errors in the use of the product in order to make corrections in good time and continue with development without the possibility of major future concerns [14].

The test carried out in the final stage of development is validation, as it is characterised by being a more quantitative check, which assesses the navigation aspects, whether they comply with usability, whether all the standards and norms have been met and whether they have been successfully followed throughout production, whether the functions are being carried out in accordance with what was stipulated in the initial objectives of the sketch, in short, this test visualises whether the product is really ready and its due conformities to be released and launched on the market [14].

Finally, comparison testing can be carried out throughout the development process, allowing errors to be detected and resolved. It is also possible to compare the content with other sites in order to avoid the same styles and content, and is essential for checking the effectiveness of the interface as well as serving as a reviewer at all stages of the site's preparation [14],

In this sense, we realise that usability evaluation tools are essential if web services are to be used dynamically and effectively by all citizens.

According to the verification elements presented, the one that stands out the most is the Investigation Method, which best determines, after a product has been developed and launched, how it has been developed, i.e. whether it meets all the usability principles and allows all citizens to use it equally, since its instruments are broader and make it possible not only to perceive the user's vision, but also that of the validator who, according to their analyses and interpretations, can see if the principles are really being adopted, not only through the use of the site, but also through the relationship that the user establishes with it, making it possible to verify its level of acceptability by the citizen.

2.2.3 Final considerations

Usability undoubtedly has elements that are closely related to accessibility, but this does not mean that they are unique, but rather that they complement each other. While accessibility provides elements that allow everyone to access the content, i.e. specific tools for the use of the visually impaired and individuals with reduced mobility, usability tends to develop concepts that allow the use of websites not only to be restricted to the mechanism of use, but also to be used in different ways by these users, based on the instruments offered by accessibility. In this way, as well as being accessible, the product would also be prone to various constructive interventions through the use of citizens, hence the importance of these elements being in harmony and complementing each other in a positive way, facilitating the use of the Web for all individuals, especially those with disabilities who, of course, have limitations that must be catered for.

Usability recommendations should therefore be followed in order to improve access and allow users to identify with the technology on offer, facilitating familiarisation with the content and building autonomous knowledge through the texts and content made available on the Web.

Therefore, the evaluation of the site based on checking its suitability for the usability referred to should be carried out correctly and frequently in order to check that institutions are in fact improving on this issue and offering, in addition to access for all, quality use of accessibility tools so that the user is independent and dynamic in the course of their use.

Websites and systems with adequate usability and accessibility are essential for the user to have a good experience in the virtual environment, more specifically in web tools, also relating these aspects directly to the concepts of UX (User Experience), which list instruments that demonstrate the degree of citizen satisfaction when accessing certain websites and pages, in order to meet their expectations in a broad and satisfactory way.

It is therefore essential that, as well as complying with recommendations, websites also take care to investigate the needs of their users in order to offer them a unique and innovative experience, hence the importance of being aware of new trends in design, web interface and UX, as can be seen in the topics covered below in the study.

2.3 New Web Design Trends and the Experience User Experience (UX)

There is a need among web design and information technology professionals and researchers to investigate UX in order to provide clues as to which and how resources or mechanisms can be used so that websites adapt to the demands of all types of users. Evidence of the need for such research involves interactivity on the Web.

With regard to interactivity on the Web, advances in recent years have not had a positive impact on universal access. Since the advent of the mouse, we are used to interacting with graphical web interfaces by clicking and scrolling. These are just a few examples of human-computer interaction via an input device. In the last decade, new forms of interactivity have emerged, including touchscreen interaction techniques. However, these new interaction mechanisms have not increased the UX of people who are blind because they are unable to use these devices. Hence the question: how will new trends influence universal access?

In this paper we investigate UX with a focus on responsive design. In Responsive Design, web pages are adaptable, i.e. the layout of the page adapts to the screen resolution of the user's device [88]. A more detailed description of these techniques is provided in the following subsections.

2.3.1 Fiat Design versus Skeumorphism

With regard to the new trends in Web Design, two styles are widely confronted, *Skeumorphism* and *Fiat Design.* From this perspective, *Skeumorphism*, better known as realism, is characterised by an interface designed to match its real-world counterpart [63]. This style is characterised by the use of icons that imitate real, tangible objects [39].

This design style strongly influenced interfaces in the 90s. In this last decade, *Skeumorphism* was the key design principle for Apple products. It can be seen that the applicability of this style was dominant in user interface projects until the resurgence of the *flat* style [70].

This style is still the navigation pattern of most game designs, an example of which can be seen in the interface of the game *Sniper Ghost Warrior 2,* but can also be applied to applications such as the *Cross DJ app,* the *Hipstamatic app*, and the *FlightBoard app* [63].

Fiat design, also known as flat design, is a digital design style that was widely discussed as a trend in 2013, but first appeared in web design in 2012 [74]. This style is characterised by a minimalist look, with a focus on removing all elements and extra effects from the design [74].

In this respect, *Fiat Design* has more simplistic interfaces, providing clear information in a cleaner design, with strong, vibrant colours and no depth in the images. In this way, the flat style shown in figure 2.1 can also be characterised by the absence of details such as gradients, borders and shadows. It can be seen that the main focus of flat design is information. As a result, this type of style, which is the result of creating a more simplistic look, can be seen visually in a flat form, thus exploiting white spaces with solid lines that behave like *layout* elements [74].

Because of its cleaner appearance and impact on user interaction [70], flat design has been widely adopted as a development standard in Web Design. Without a shadow of a doubt, it is currently one of the most popular approaches to

Figure 2.1: *Example of a flat design interface. Federal University of Alagoas (UFAL).*

adopted by *designers* when constructing web *layouts* [74]. As a result, the vast majority of professionals saw flat design as an opportunity to create simple, good-looking web pages.

2.3.2 Responsive Web Design

With the advance of technologies and the evolution of devices experienced in the last decade, anyone can easily surf the web from any device: phone, *tablet,* mobile phone, games console, television or PC [88]. All of these devices have the ability to connect to the Internet with their own screen dimensions in different resolutions. This last factor is what has motivated the professional and scientific community to research the creation of adaptive design.

The term Responsive Web Design was coined in 2010 in a report published on the "A *list apart"* portal by Ethan Marcotte [54]. Then, a year later, the term became a trend in web interface design.

Responsive Design, in general, can be defined as a way of making websites more adaptable, i.e. websites can be easily viewed and used on any type of device. For any device, the screen size will adapt the site to fit the screen [72], Figure 2.2 illustrates the same interface for different media on the Web.

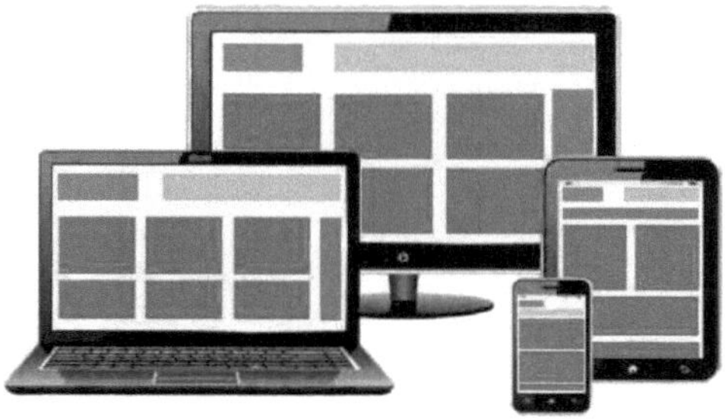

Figure 2.2: *Interface for different media on the Web [62].*

Website development must include practices that influence the success of a Web Design project [72]. This means that today there is a need to create design strategies that respond to content, an approach that allows application content to adapt easily to any device.

With this, it is possible to create an application that is easy to use, thus reducing the cost of website development [62]. The following characteristics are known as Responsive Design best practices, having an impact on user perception.

- In order to make the interface more user-friendly, the number of *layout* columns should change according to the user's screen resolution;
- The content offered by the layout should be presented according to context, i.e. menus and content should be prioritised based on importance from the user's perspective;
- All images and videos should be automatically resized to the size of the screen display;
- *HTML* content, images, *CSS* and *JavaScripts* should be cached to save the user's internet usage;
- The execution of data synchronisation should be imperceptible to the user, thus running in the background. Providing a better user experience;
- The spaces between elements, such as links, should extend their width so that they don't accidentally touch smaller devices.

While in the last decade some technologies have been close to extinction, for example *Flash,* new standards are on the rise in web *layout* construction, for example *CSS3* and *HTML5* [60]. Responsive Design uses these resources to achieve portability between different devices. Consequently, while *HTML5* structures all the content of the *layout, CSS3* will tell the browser how to interpret it [72].

```
@media only screen and (max-width: 720px){
        .site-logo, .site-nav{float:none;}
        .site-nav li{margin: 0.5em;}
}

@media only screen and (max-width: 500px){
        html{font-size: 14px;}
}

@media only screen and (max-width: 460px){
        .grid-cell {width: 100%}
}

@media only screen and (max-width: 420px){
        html(font-size: 13px;}
        h1 {font-size: 2.5em;}
}
```

Figure 2.3: *Example of Media Queries [71].*

Therefore, one of the defining elements of Responsive Design is *Media Queries. Media Queries* are the attributes that make context-sensitive websites respond to devices with the appropriate application resolution [72]. Previously, *CSS* was used to build web pages without taking into account the screen resolution of the users making the request. Now, the concepts of *Media Queries* are used. *Media Queries* allow us to create different styles for different device screen sizes. In this way, the web page is displayed using the style that best suits the desired dimensions [88].

We realise that Responsive Design is a new way of applying existing elements, building style markup declarations and *HTML* code to achieve the objectives of applications, making them more responsive.

2.3.3 User Experience

At the end of the last century, user experience became a jargon in the field of design [77]. According to Yang (2014), UX is "understood as a set of sensations, feelings or emotional responses that occur when users interact with a system" [106]. Unlike usability, which can have objective criteria for evaluation, UX essentially encompasses subjective criteria [89].

For many researchers and professionals in the field of Human-Computer Interface, one of the most important motivations in the field of user experience is concern for the quality of the software product [41]. UX is an instrument for dealing with user expectations in web applications through evaluations of partial or total effects on user interactions with the applications. As well as encompassing usability principles, UX also involves the emotional aspects of users [41]. In addition to emotional impact, UX includes effects such as aesthetics, convenience, novelty and originality [41],

Usability addresses the aspects of effectiveness and efficiency; productivity and ease of use; learning capacity and retention capacity; as well as the subjective aspects of user satisfaction. Usability deals with the pragmatic aspects of UX, while utility is a component of UX that enables the functional usability of the system, thus fulfilling the goal for which it was developed [55].

UX requires new techniques for evaluating user perceptions on an ongoing basis throughout its life cycle, since the initial experience can be determined by aesthetic perceptions. Subsequent evaluation is dependent on the interaction process, usability and usefulness of the application [89].

There is a lot of research aimed at investigating the user experience in web, desktop and *mobile* applications. Thus, in 2013, at the *ACM Conference on Human Factors in Computing Systems (IHC) Workshop,* 18 papers were presented on the subject of "Human-Computer Interface", of which around 45% dealt with UX in textual form, while the rest discussed the importance of usability and User-Centred Design (UCD) [51].

Consequently, with this conceptual shift from usability to UX, new challenges arise among HCI professionals to deal with this expansion of interaction design [51].

2.3.4 Final considerations

With the advance in access to technology by different users on different devices, new trends are emerging in web design. These include the way in which the *layout of* web applications adapts to the context of users' devices.

Other trends are related to design styles on the web, for example *Fiat Design,* which has minimalist elements that give a cleaner and more impactful appearance when interacting with the user.

In the last decade, UX has emerged as a jargon in the field of web design. Thus, UX can be understood as a set of emotional responses during user interactions with systems.

It should be noted that the methods used by UX are based on consolidated Usability work. However, it seems that there is a gap in the UX literature.

new design trends on the Web. Chapter 3 therefore presents a systematically detailed review that confirms this hypothesis.

CHAPTER 3

Systematic Literature Review

This chapter presents a systematic review of the literature on user experience (UX), considering a comparison between visually impaired, blind and sighted users, focusing on scientific articles published in the last five years, from January 2009 to January 2015.

One possible hypothesis is that there are no scientific studies evaluating the impact of new web trends on user experience (UX). In this context, the following questions were designed to guide the research:

- Q01 - Can you tell from the existing literature what the differences and similarities are in the user experience of new web trends between blind and sighted users?
- Q02 - Can you tell from the existing literature how relevant the study of user experience is to new web trends among blind and sighted users?

In order to search and classify the research for the purpose of answering questions Q01 and Q02, each reference included in this review was grouped into one of the categories shown in figure 3.1. These categories can obtain objective results that are extracted directly from the studies or subjective results that are obtained through the reviewer's conclusions and analyses.

Therefore, the studies included in the analysis of the articles were grouped as follows:

- G01 - Addresses the relevance of UX to new trends on the Web;
- G02 - Addresses the relevance of UX applied to visually impaired or blind users;
- G03 - Addresses the relevance of UX in new Web trends applied to visually impaired users;
- G04 - Addresses the relevance of UX in new Web trends applied to the visually impaired or blind users;

Figure 3.1: *Hierarchy of category classification (UX).*

- G05 - Addresses other UX issues applied to the visually impaired or blind users;
- G06 - Addresses other UX issues applied to new trends on the Web;
- G07 - Addresses other relevant UX issues;

This classification was carried out when the keywords and abstracts of the articles were visible during the execution of the protocol or made available through careful reading to find such a classification. For example, articles retrieved from the database without an abstract but which had keywords on UX. In this case, it was necessary to read the article more carefully in an attempt to find approaches to the relevance of UX, new trends on the Web or subjects that deal with UX applied to the visually impaired or blind.

The following subsections detail the methodology used to plan, identify, select and extract the results found in the systematic literature review.

3.1 Planning the Systematic Review

This section discusses the construction of the research protocol, the selection of sources and the selection criteria for the studies identified in the literature.

3.1.1 Search string

In order to guide the search for evidence in the literature, considering the research questions, some key words were extracted to create a set of three protocols, which can be adapted according to the search engine of each source:

- PI - (User Experience AND UX);

- P2 - ("User Experience" AND "UX");
- P3 - ("Web" AND ("Blind" OR "Visually Impaired" OR "non-blind") AND ("User Experience") AND ("UX")).

3.1.2 Research Sources

The research was carried out between November 2014 and January 2015 on the following databases:

- IEEE Xplore Digital Library;
- Scopus;
- Science Direct;
- Springer;
- Google Scholar.

The searches were configured to bring up the results of articles in English, as this is the standard language for international publications.

3.1.3 Selection Criteria

After constructing the search protocol and choosing the sources for the research, the results obtained should be analysed in order to find their relevance. For this primary categorisation of studies, the following inclusion criteria will be adopted:

i Scientific studies that address the relevance of UX;

ii Scientific studies that address other UX issues.

However, it was necessary to create criteria for excluding articles from the study. The criteria adopted were:

i Scientific studies that only address Usability and Accessibility issues outside the context of UX;
ii Scientific studies that address UX issues in products not related to HCI or Computing;
iii Scientific studies that don't address UX issues;
iv Scientific studies containing key words such as "UX" and "User Experience", but outside the context of this research.

3.2 Identification of studies

The search was divided into three parts (El, E2 and E3) in order to find studies to answer the research questions (Q01 and Q02). The searches were divided according to the Pl, P2 and P3 protocols. The following subsections explain the executions with the graphs resulting from the identification of this study.

3.2.1 First run (El)

After defining the search *strings* in subsection 3.1.1, the Pl protocol was run, separating it by research source (subsection 3.1.2). The search was carried out over time, i.e. separating the results of the studies by year of publication (2009 to 2015) as shown in figure 3.2.

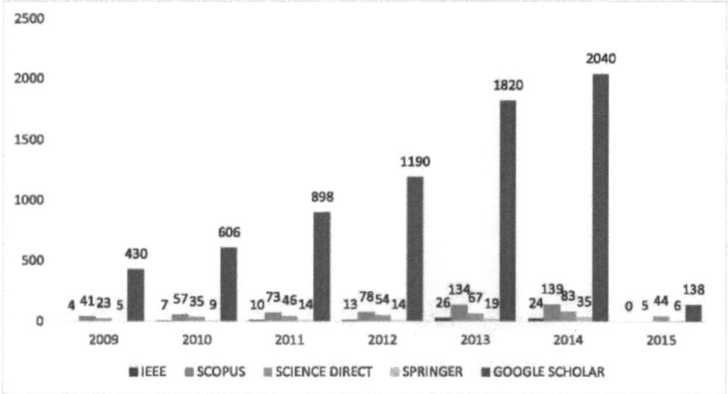

Figure 3.2: *Result of running the Pl protocol by year of article publication.*

Running the Pl protocol in the first round, 8,187 references were retrieved, 84 of which came from the *IEEE Xplore Digital Library,* 527 from *Scopus*, 352 from *Science Direct,* 102 from *Springer* and 7,122 from *Google Scholar* (figure 3.2).

We realised that there is a high percentage of publications in *Google Scholar,* around 86% of all publications. After making this observation, we realised that in the selection phase this rate could decrease, since the vast majority of other research sources *(IEEE, Scopus, Springer* and *Science Direct)* are also indexed by *Google Scholar,* thus duplicating or rejecting work according to the criteria set out in subsection 3.1.3.

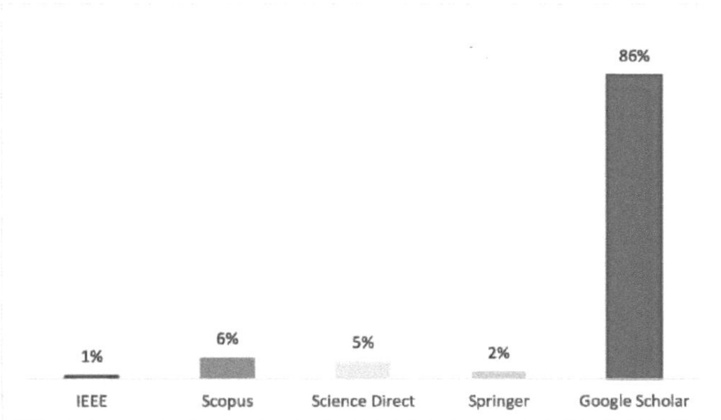

Figure 3.3: *Percentage of Pl protocol execution results by research source.*

3.2.2 Second Run (E2)

The aim of run E2 was to refine the search run (El). To do this, the P2 protocol was used, respecting the criteria already used in the first runs (El). Figure 3.4 shows the results of the studies in this run, separated by the year of publication.

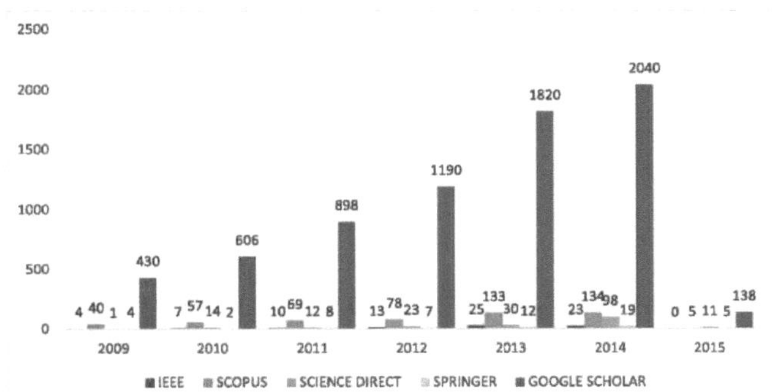

Figure 3.4: *Result of running the P2 protocol by year of publication of the articles.*

When running the P2 protocol in the second round, 7,966 references were retrieved, of which 82 articles came from the *IEEE Xplore Digital Library,* 516 from *Scopus*, 189 from *Science Direct,* 57 from *Springer* and 7,122 from *Google Scholar* (figure 3.4). It can be seen that there was a decrease of around 2.7 per cent in the results found compared to the results of the El run, but that this percentage did not affect the final results of the P2 protocol.

It can be concluded that run E2 was not very effective in terms of delimiting the Pl protocol, since the vast majority of the studies found in run E2 may be contained in the results of run El, thus duplicating studies. Figure 3.5 shows the results of run E2 by research source with their respective percentage.

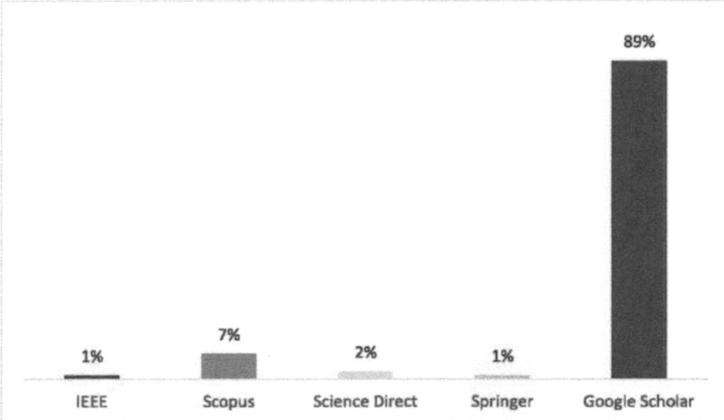

Figure 3.5: *Percentage of P2 protocol execution results by research source.*

3.2.3 Third Execution (E3)

In run E3, the aim was to carry out a careful search of the results, aligning UX and Web Accessibility studies. To this end, the P3 protocol was used, respecting the criteria already used in the first runs (El). Figure 3.6 shows the results of the studies in this run.

Running the P3 protocol in the third round, 479 references were retrieved, 82 of which came from the *IEEE Xplore Digital Library,* 16 from *Scopus*, 232 from *Science Direct,* 113 from *Springer* and 36 from *Google Scholar* (figure 3.6).

In this round, we can see that there was a decrease of around 94% (ninety-four per cent) in the results found in relation to the results of run E2. As a result, we can conclude that run E3 was more effective in relation to the delimitation of the P2 protocol, yielding results that are close to questions Q01 and Q02. Figure 3.7 shows the results of run E3 by search source with their respective percentage.

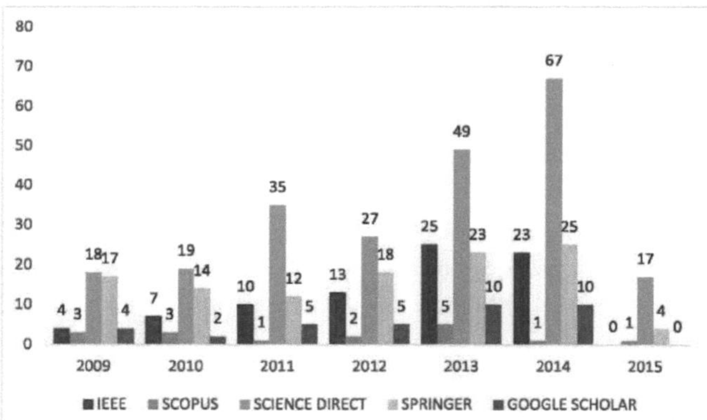

Figure 3.6: *Result of running protocol P3 by year of publication of the articles.*

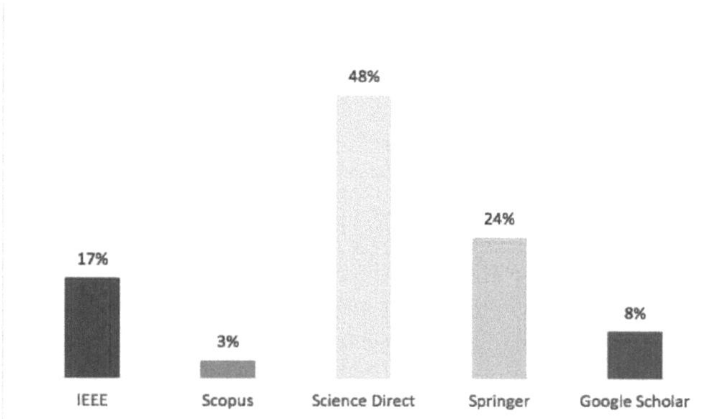

Figure 3.7: *Percentage of protocol execution results P3 by research source.*

3.3 Study selection

The aim of selecting the studies was to carry out a primary categorisation of the results found when identifying the studies by applying the inclusion and exclusion criteria listed in subsection 3.1.3. This primary categorisation focused on the final results of the El, E2 and E3 runs. Table 3.1 shows the quantitative results of the identification of studies (subsection 3.2) carried out by the Pl, P2 and P3 protocols. With the sum of the results found in the execution of the Pl, P2 and P3 protocols, a total of 16,632 (sixteen thousand six hundred and thirty-two) articles were analysed.

Table 3.1: *Total number of articles identified in the research.*

	2009	2010	2011	2012	2013	2014	2015	Total
PI	503	714	1041	1349	2066	2321	193	8187
P2	479	686	997	1311	2020	2314	159	7966
P3	46	45	63	65	112	126	22	479

results by applying the inclusion and exclusion criteria described in subsection 3.1.3. Three more categories were created to classify the results:

i Duplicate articles;
ii Discarded articles (using exclusion criteria);
iv Accepted articles (using the inclusion criteria).

The articles were analysed by period and research source (Subsection 3.1.2), i.e. a set of articles was selected for each specific year of publication (2009, 2010, 2011, 2012, 2013, 2014 and 2015), thus accounting for the analysis by period. The selection was made by carefully reading the content of the articles' abstracts, titles and keywords. In this sense, some articles required a more in-depth reading in order to find some of the aspects listed in the classification criteria. For better explanation, the following sub-sections present the form and result of the selection and identification of the studies found with the execution of the protocols.

1.1.1 Exclusion of Duplicate Studies

The exclusion of duplicate articles was carried out automatically with the support of specific software to help carry out systematic reviews *(Start Tool).* The *Start Tool* software was created by the Software Engineering Research Laboratory (LaPES) of the Department of Computing at the Federal University of São Carlos (DC/UFSCar) [94]. Table 3.2 illustrates the number of articles that were found with "duplicate" status in the search.

Table 3.2: *Total number of duplicate articles in the search.*

2009	2010	2011	2012	2013	2014	2015	Total
561	801	1166	1493	2304	2580	222	9127

As Table 3.2 shows, 9,127 (nine thousand one hundred and twenty-seven) duplicate articles were found in rounds El, E2, E3 in the study identification phase. This figure represents around 55% (fifty-five per cent) of the total number of articles researched in this study. The high rate of duplicate articles is justified by the large number of articles found in the El, E2 and E3 runs on the *Google Scholar* database, which indexed the other articles found in the other research sources *(IEEE, Scopus, Science Direct and Springer).*

1.1.2 Exclusion of Rejected Studies

For this analysis and classification, in addition to using the software mentioned above in subsection 3.3.1, a careful reading was carried out in order to find elements that would allow such classifications. These elements, such as abstracts, titles, keywords and content, were classified according to the selection and exclusion criteria in subsection 3.1.3:

- Scientific studies that deal only with Usability and Accessibility issues outside the context of UX;
- Scientific studies that address UX issues in products not related to HCI or Computing;
- Scientific studies that don't address UX issues;
- Scientific studies containing key words such as "UX" and "User Experience", but outside the context of this research.

Table 3.3 illustrates the number of articles that were analysed and classified as "rejected" in this research.

Table 3.3: *Total number of articles rejected in the survey.*

2009	2010	2011	2012	2013	2014	2015	Total
407	566	843	1135	1592	1769	117	6429

As shown in Table 3.3, 16,632 (sixteen thousand six hundred and thirty-two) articles were analysed in rounds El, E2, E3 resulting from the study identification phase, of which 6,429 (six thousand four hundred and twenty-nine) articles were rejected for not meeting the exclusion criteria listed in this research. We believe that this percentage of articles, around 39% (thirty-nine per cent) of the rejection rate, was due to the fact that UX is a multidisciplinary term and can therefore be used in various studies that are not related to the area of HCI [88].

1.1.3 Accepted Studies

The inclusion of the studies accepted in the research adopted the same method of analysis applied in subsection 3.3.2. The inclusion criteria were used to carry out this analysis and classification. The inclusion criteria used were:

- Scientific studies that address the relevance of UX;
- Scientific studies that address other UX issues.

This classification helped construct the primary categorisation of the articles accepted in the research, shown in figure 3.1 (Hierarchy of the classification of UX categories). Table 3.4 illustrates the number of articles that were analysed and classified with "accepted" status.

Table 3.4: *Total articles accepted in the research.*

2009	2010	2011	2012	2013	2014	2015	Total
62	72	89	86	280	391	35	1015

As shown in Table 3.4, 1,015 (one thousand and fifteen) articles were accepted by applying the selection criteria in rounds El, E2 and E3, resulting from the study identification phase. These articles were classified as "accepted" because they met the selection (inclusion) criteria listed in this research. Figure 3.8 shows the number of articles that were analysed and classified as "rejected", "duplicated" and "accepted".

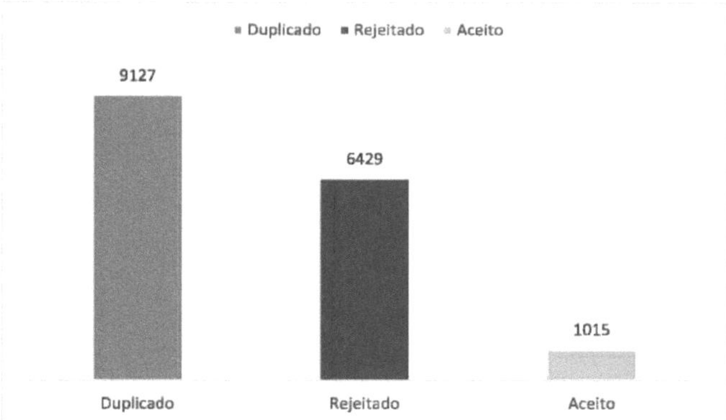

Figure 3.8: *Number of articles in the survey by classification.*

The extraction of the results classified as "accepted", around 6.1% (six point one per cent), will be discussed in section 3.4 (Results).

3.4 Results

In sections 3.1, 3.2 and 3.3, we described the process of preparing the systematic review and the stages of carrying out the searches (El, E2 and E3) and selecting the results. In this section, we will try to extract the data collected and classified in subsection 3.3.3 (accepted studies). In order to assess and summarise the articles that have already been classified, the following main categories are used (figure 3.1):

3.4.1 It addresses the relevance of UX;

II. Addresses other UX issues.

After the primary extraction and categorisation, new sub-categorisations were carried out in order to meet the objective of identifying and analysing the scientific papers to show the originality and relevance of investigating the UX of the visually impaired, taking into account the new trends on the Web *(Fiat Design,* Responsive Design and Web Accessibility). To this end, the following subsection presents the results of the extraction and summarisation of this research.

3.4.1 Results of Categories I and II

In the classification process carried out in the results selection phase, around 6.1% (six point one per cent) of the total number of articles were identified that could be grouped into categories I and II. In this respect, the first summarisation of the results assessed 1,015 (one thousand and fifteen) papers, which were extracted and categorised. Figure 3.9 shows this grouping with the total number of articles in the categories separated by year of publication.

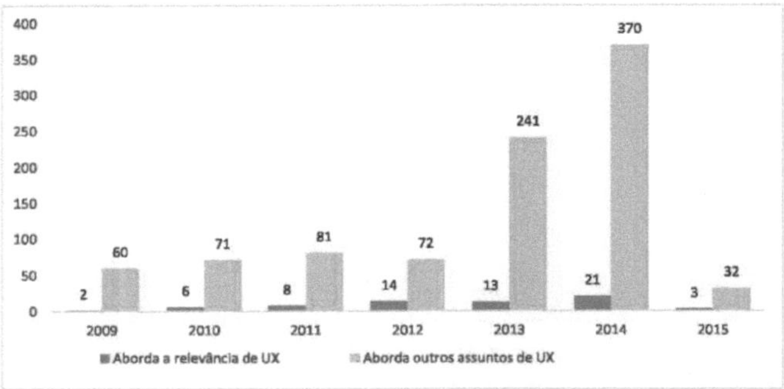

Figure 3.9: *Summarising the results of categories I and II.*

The graph shown in figure 3.9 summarises 67 (sixty-seven) articles grouped in category I and 927 articles grouped in category II.

3.4.2 Studies Addressing Other UX Issues

We found a large number of publications in category n, around 91.3% (ninety-one point three per cent) of the total number of articles, which deal with other relevant UX issues. It was therefore decided to apply refinement to this category. The following subcategories were used to carry out the reclassification:

i. Studies applied to the visually impaired or blind users;

ii. Studies applied to new web trends - Fiat Design and Responsive Design;

iii. Studies that address other relevant UX issues.

Figure 3.10 shows the results after subcategorising (i, ii and iii) category II.

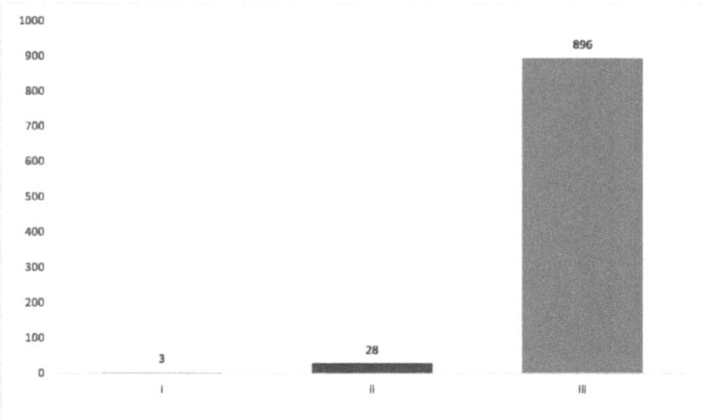

Figure 3.10: *Summarisation of results according to the criteria set out in (i), (ii) and (iii) - Category II.*

Figure 3.10 summarises the reclassification of the results. Of the total of 927 (nine hundred and twenty-seven) articles found in category II, 896 (eight hundred and ninety-six) articles address other relevant UX issues, 28 (twenty-eight) articles are related to studies applied to new Web trends. There is a scarcity of studies applied to the visually impaired or blind users that address other UX issues, in this research only 3 (three) articles were found that contemplate this aspect. Figure 3.11 shows the percentage of reclassified articles.

3.4.3 Studies Addressing the Relevance of UX

After reclassifying the studies dealing with other UX issues under category II, we went on to apply the same reclassification process to the studies dealing with the relevance of UX under category I. Sixty-seven (67) articles were extracted from this category and refined using the following subcategories:

i. Studies that address the relevance of UX in new Web trends applied to the visually impaired or blind users;
ii. Studies that address the relevance of UX in new Web trends applied to sighted users;

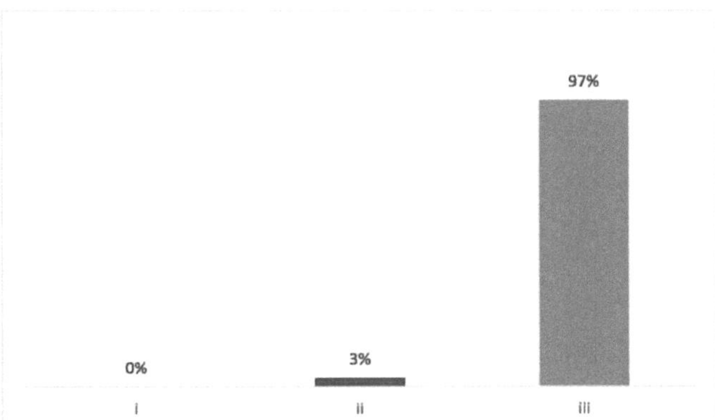

Figure 3.11: *Percentage of results summarised according to the criteria set out in (i), (ii) and (iii) - Category II.*

iii. Studies that address the relevance of UX for visually impaired or blind users.

Figure 3.12 shows the results after subcategorising (i, ii and iii) category I.

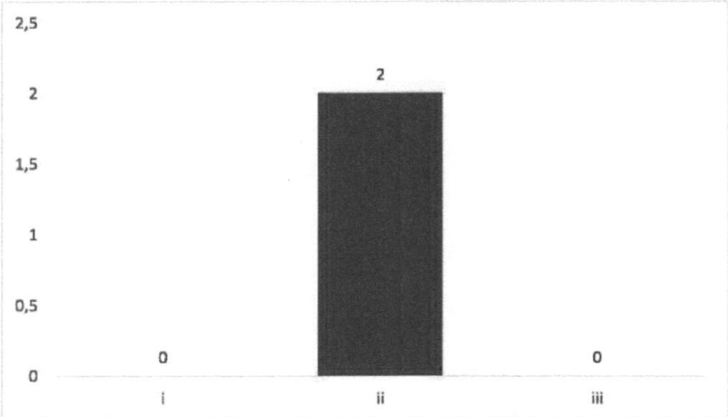

Figure 3.12: *Summarisation of results (i, ii and iii) - Category I.*

Figure 3.12 shows the summary of the reclassification of results I (Addresses the relevance of UX). Of the total of 67 (sixty-seven) articles found in category I, 02 (two) articles are studies that address the relevance of UX for visually impaired or blind users. The remaining 65 (sixty-five) articles were not reclassified in subcategories (i) and (iii). We observed that the vast majority, around 97 per cent (ninety-seven per cent) of the articles only covered the relevance of UX, but the studies did not address the relevance of UX in new Web trends applied to visually impaired or blind users, nor the relevance of UX in new Web trends applied to sighted users.

3.4.4 Final Extraction Result

After extracting the studies identified in section 3.2 (Identification of Studies) and applying the reclassification process in subsections 3.4.2 (Studies Addressing Other UX Issues) and 3.4.3 (Studies Addressing UX Relevance), the final set of analysed studies was obtained. Table 3.5 shows the final grouping of these studies.

Table 3.5: *Total articles accepted in the survey by category.*

Final Extraction Result by Grouping	Articles
G01 - Addresses the relevance of UX to new trends on the Web.	0
G02 - Addresses the relevance of UX applied to visually impaired or blind users.	2
G03 - Addresses the relevance of UX in new Web trends applied to visually impaired users.	0
G04 - Addresses the relevance of UX in new Web trends applied to the visually impaired or blind users.	0
G05 - Addresses other UX issues applied to the visually impaired or blind	3

users.	
G06 - Addresses other UX issues applied to new trends on the Web.	28
G07 - Addresses other relevant UX issues.	896

3.5 Discussions

By extracting and analysing the papers, it was possible to group and subcategorise the results in order to identify and analyse scientific studies published in the last five years to show the originality and relevance of investigating UX for the visually impaired, taking into account new trends on the Web. To this end, this systematic review has made it possible to construct a relevant overview of UX aspects. In this sense, the results include some of the subcategories that were created by extracting terms from questions Q1 and Q2 of the survey.

The first question Q1 (Can you tell from the existing literature what the differences and similarities are in the user experience of new web trends between blind and sighted users?) aimed to find UX papers that addressed any of the aspects listed in subsection 2.3 (new web design trends and user experience (UX)). To this end, we found and analysed articles that were grouped under the following headings:

a) They addressed other aspects of UX applied to visually impaired or blind users (3 articles);
b) They addressed other UX issues applied to new web trends (28 articles);
c) They addressed other UX issues (896 articles).

Around 97% (ninety-seven per cent) of the total number of articles that dealt with other UX issues were classified as relevant after analysis. Table 3.6 shows the most recurrent subjects found from the perspective of relevant UX approaches.

Table 3.6: *Recurring themes from the survey on relevant UX issues.*

The Most Frequently Asked Questions
UX methods applied to mobile (LeanUX).
UX Agile approach.
Measuring UX in web services.
Usability techniques in UX.
UX measures applied to gamification
User-centred design (UX).
UX, products and the software industry (organisational models).

However, studies of UX applied to the visually impaired or blind users were found [107, 109, 108], but no studies comparing UX between blind and sighted users were found among these articles (3 articles). However, in terms of addressing new trends on the Web, the studies did not correlate UX with blind, visually impaired or sighted users.

The second question Q2 (From the existing literature, what is the relevance of studying user experience in the new web trends among blind and visually impaired users?) aimed to find UX papers that addressed the relevance of investigating UX applied to the aspects listed in subsection 2.3 (new web design trends and user experience (UX)). In this sense, 69 (sixty-nine) articles were classified and analysed, of which only 2 (two) addressed the relevance of UX applied to blind or visually impaired users (Web Accessibility) [40, 10]. The vast majority of the articles classified in this category addressed the relevance of investigating UX, but did not correlate this approach with new trends on the Web applied to users with disabilities visual, blind or sighted.

Therefore, by extracting and analysing the results (existing literature) it was not possible to know what the differences and similarities in user experience are

on new web trends among blind and visually impaired users. However, it was possible to identify the relevance of the study of UX to blind or visually impaired users, but that research into this aspect, relating to new trends on the Web *(Fiat Design* and Responsive Design) with blind and sighted users is still a field of UX research to be investigated.

3.6 Final considerations

In this systematic review, 16,571 articles on UX were identified, analysed and classified according to the inclusion and exclusion criteria, investigating the impact of new web trends on the experience of blind, visually impaired and sighted users. The evaluation aimed to answer research questions Ql and Q2 through a careful analysis of the studies identified, extracted and categorised.

By categorising the research results into studies that address the relevance of UX or studies that address other UX issues, it was possible to partially answer question Ql (From the existing literature, can you tell what the differences and similarities are in the user experience of new web trends between blind and sighted users?) and Q2 (From the existing literature, can you tell what the relevance is of studying the user experience of new web trends between blind and sighted users?). In this sense, the hypothesis raised at the beginning of this chapter was confirmed by the lack of scientific studies evaluating the impact of new web trends on user experience (UX), thus showing the originality and relevance of investigating the UX of the visually impaired, considering new web trends.

Therefore, this systematic review makes a positive contribution to breaking new ground in UX research, emphasising the importance of current studies that relate the three important perspectives on the web: web accessibility, UX and new web trends. Chapter 4 therefore presents a detailed case study that addresses these three perspectives.

CHAPTER 4

Case Study

This chapter proposes a case study on the experience of blind and partially sighted users on new web trends, comparing UX on responsive and non-responsive sites. This chapter is organised as follows:

- Subsection 4.1 describes the sample used in the research;
- Subsection 4.2 presents the process of selecting websites for the research, using selection criteria and applying accessibility tests;
- Subsection 4.3 describes the instruments and procedures used to collect the data;
- Subsection 4.4 describes the procedures used to analyse the data;
- Subsection 4.5 contains the final considerations;

4.1 Research Sample

According to Nielsen (2000), some people think that usability is an expensive and complex process, but this is not true [67]. Thus, good usability results can be achieved with approximately twenty users to carry out the tests, obtaining statistically significant numbers for quantitative studies [65].

Thus, by collecting usability test data from a single user, it is possible to identify a third of an application's usability problems, but when we analyse the other users, we realise that there is overlapping information and, in addition, new problems are identified [67].

It can be seen that this sample survey can be defined by the set of users that are used in an exploratory survey. According to Gil (2010), "the conclusions obtained from this sample are projected to the entire universe, taking into account the margin of error, which is obtained through statistical calculations" [36].

The sample for this study was made up of two sets of users with nine participants each. One set of sighted users **(who can see)** and one set of blind users (acquired or congenital blindness). A blind user is a person with total blindness, i.e. it is assumed that the person has complete loss of vision or zero vision [24],

The research was carried out with the help of the Brazilian Centre for Rehabilitation and Support for the Visually Impaired (CEBRAV), located at Rua 29 A, Quadra 66, Lote E, Número 53, Centro. Goiânia-Goiás.

4.2 Selection of Websites

Unlike the study presented by Nielsen (2000), who carried out usability tests on 25 websites in different genres with a wide variety of design styles [67], this study looks at carrying out UX tests on specific groups, both in terms of style and genre.

In this case study, 165 (one hundred and sixty-five) websites were identified, grouped into three categories: education, e-commerce and entertainment. We analysed 107 (one hundred and seven) websites that fell into the education category, specifically the federal education network in Brazil, which is made up of the Federal Institutes of Education, Science and Technology, the Federal Technological University of Paraná and the Federal Universities. The full list of websites in this category can be seen in Appendix A.l.

In the e-commerce category, a list of 42 (forty-two) websites was analysed. The analyses were carried out on an exploratory basis, i.e. searches were carried out for websites that fell into this category, using the *google* search tool. The full list of websites in this category can be seen in Appendix A.2.

In the entertainment category, 16 (sixteen) websites were analysed. In this respect, research was carried out focussing on the profile of blind users, since the tasks were carried out by a heterogeneous set of users. The full list of websites in this category can be seen in Appendix A.3.

4.2.1 Selection Criteria

As this was a heterogeneous sample of users, certain criteria were used to select the websites.

The first criterion is related to the accessibility compliance level of the applications, i.e. websites must have an accessibility level equal to or greater than 5.5 (five point five), according to the WCAG 2.0 accessibility guidelines. Identifying the level of accessibility can be done through accessibility tests using automatic tools, such as the *AccessMonitor* tool.

The second criterion is linked to the aim of this research. In each category, one responsive and one non-responsive website should be chosen in order to make comparisons between the two design styles, but the accessibility index between the two websites should not differ by more than 0.5.

Finally, at least one of the two websites in each category must feature *Fiat Design* elements.

4.2.2 Accessibility Test

According to Sydik (2007), for content to be accessible, the first step is for it to be compatible with accessibility standards. Accessibility support technologies need to be able to analyse content correctly, so it is essential that websites are better designed [90]. With this in mind, the use of automatic validators can help to build more accessible websites from the project conception stage right through to when they are made available.

Accessibility tests were therefore carried out using an automatic validator that checks websites for compliance with the WCAG 1.0 and WCAG 2.0 guidelines. The tool used to carry out the tests was *AccessMonitor*[3] . Figure 4.1 shows the application of the accessibility test on the website of the Federal University of Alagoas using the *AccessMonitor* tool.

The test consists of entering the website's *URL* into the automatic accessibility validator, which will issue a report describing the evaluation index and the errors found according to the WCAG 2.0 priority level.

Appendix A shows the results of the tests applied to websites in the education, e-commerce and entertainment categories. The tables show the lists of websites with their respective accessibility indices.

[3]www.acessibilidade.gov.pt/accessmonitor

4.2.3 Selection results

After analysing the websites according to the selection criteria (subsection 4.2.1), the results were grouped into two subcategories: responsive and non-responsive designs. Table 4.1 shows the set of websites that met the criteria stipulated in subsection 4.2.1, grouped into the education, e-commerce and entertainment categories.

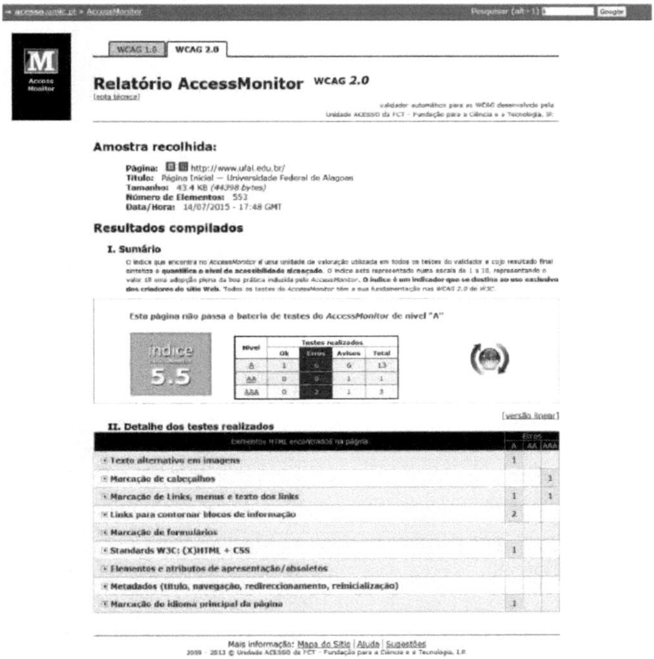

Figure 4.1: *Accessibility test on the UFAL website using the AccessMonitor tool.*

Table 4.1: *Set of websites selected for the research.*

Category	Design	Website	index
Education	Responsive	www.ufal.br (SOI)	5.7
Education	Not responsive	www.ufsc.br (S02)	5.8
e-Commerce	Responsive	www.shopfato.com.br (S03)	6.3
e-Commerce	Not responsive	www.fundacaodorina.org.br (S04)	6.4
Entertainment	Responsive	www.legendasonora.com.br (S05)	6.5
Entertainment	Not responsive	www.midiace.com.br (S06)	6.1

As table 4.1 shows, the websites of the Federal University of Alagoas and the Federal University of Santa Catarina have accessibility indices greater than or equal to 5.5, the former being classified as responsive, with *Fiat Design* elements. The Shopfato and Dorina Nowill Foundation e-commerce websites also have accessibility indices greater than or equal to 5.5, the former being classified as responsive.

In the entertainment category, the Legenda Sonora and Midiace websites also have accessibility ratings greater than or equal to 5.5, the former being classified as responsive and with *Fiat Design* elements, as well as being the winner of the 3rd edition of the Todos @ Web Award organised by W3C Brazil in partnership with the Ministry of Planning's Secretariat for Logistics and Information Technology, the Secretariat for the Rights of People with Disabilities and the Association for Assistance to Disabled Children [99].

4.3 Data Collection Instruments and Procedures

According to Prodanov and Freitas (2013), the definition of the instruments for collecting data in a research project will depend on the objectives that the researcher intends to achieve and the universe to be researched [76]. According to Lakatos and Marconi (2003), there are several procedures that can be used to collect research data, which vary according to the type of investigation [49]. Generally speaking, in usability tests, in addition to the application of tasks, the techniques of observation, interviews and questionnaires are also used.

Therefore, in order to carry out UX tests, it is essential to apply user interaction tasks. According to Maule (2012), the basic reason for carrying out tests with users is to find out whether they understand the purpose of the website and whether they can carry out such interactions [55].

In this work, scenarios and tasks were created to carry out user tests. Data was collected by applying usability and UX questionnaires. To analyse the performance of each user, systematic observation techniques were used, analysing the time and possible barriers faced during interactions.

4.3.1 Scenarios and Tasks

For the UX and usability tests, it was proposed that specific tasks be carried out for each category of website, so that each user had knowledge of a specific scenario, carrying out a set of tasks within each scenario. According to Nielsen and Loranger (2007), this is the way most usability tests are conducted and is an excellent technique for discovering how the design elements of a website work [68].

According to Nielsen (2000), the tasks should be sufficient to assess how well the sites support the most typical objectives that users have when visiting them [67]. Thus, in the education category, two scenarios were proposed with three tasks in each. In the e-commerce and entertainment category, one scenario was proposed for each, with six tasks in each scenario

The following subsections present the scenarios with their respective tasks for each category of website, in responsive and non-responsive design.

4.3.1.1 Education Category

Scenario 1 - You are a student interested in applying to a university, you are interested in information about the admission process, as well as information such as the location of the university, as will be presented in the Tasks:

- Task 1 - Find where the university is located and its address.
- Task 2 - Find an e-mail or a page to contact the University to comment on or report a problem with the

site.

- Task 3 - Find out the first deadline for submitting to the selection process.

Scenario 2 - You are a student on the Computer Engineering course at this university and you want to access some information or search for some information that you need, such as access to the university's *webmail*, the course's pedagogical project, the academic calendar; as will be presented in the Tasks:

- Task 4 - Find out where the Pedagogical Project for the Computer Engineering course is.
- Task 5 - Find out where the academic calendar is and when classes are due to start next term.
- Task 6 - Find the University's webmail login page and try to log in.

4.3.1.2 e-Commerce category

Scenario 3 - You are interested in buying something new and have to look for information about the product you want to buy, as well as the price and payment methods:

- Task 7 - Find the address of this shop.
- Task 8 - Add the first item you find to the basket and try to close the order.
- Task 9 - After making a purchase, you need to contact the company, find the telephone number.
- Task 10 - Register your e-mail address to receive news from the site or the newsletter.
- Task 11 - Try making a new purchase, but change the quantity of the object purchased to 05 units before finalising the purchase.
- Task 12 - Tell us which social networks this website is on.

4.3.1.3 Entertainment category

Scenario 4 - You are a user looking for audio-described videos and are interested in some videos and particular information about each project/website:

- Task 13 - Find out which social networks the website is on.
- Task 14 - Watch at least 30 seconds of the first video you come across.
- Task 15 - Name 5 titles from the portfolio of videos/films that have already been audiodescribed by the site.
- Task 16 - Carry out a search on your own site for the term "Cinderella".
- Task 17 - Find an e-mail address available on the website to send a message if necessary.
- Task 18 - Fill in the contact form and send us your opinion of the site.

4.3.2 UX questionnaires

In this case study, the aim of the UX questionnaires was to assess users' feelings about a given set of tasks, thus studying the hedonic and pragmatic dimensions of UX. Pragmatic aspects of UX are understood to include, in addition to usability, the emotional attributes felt by users during interactions with a given system [41]. In this sense, emotional impact is the affective component of UX, which helps to analyse users' feelings. Two UX questionnaires were used for this purpose. The *Affect Grid* questionnaire (Appendix D) and the

PANAS questionnaire (Appendix E).

The *Affect Grid* is a UX tool that makes it possible to classify the emotional aspects felt by users during interactions [81]. This tool consists of a questionnaire and a grid. The questionnaire uses an objective question to identify the emotions felt by users, for example, how the user felt when carrying out the proposed task. When answering, the user chooses a score on a scale of 1 to 9 - (displeasure to pleasure) - (X axis) and a score, also on a scale of 1 to 9 - (sleepy to excited) - (Y axis). It can be seen from this question that users are aware of only four attributes: displeasure, pleasure, sleepy and excited. Once this answer has been collected, the intersection between the scores provided by the user on the X-axis and the Y-axis is counted in a space on the grid. For example, if a user provides a score of 7 for displeasure-pleasure (X-axis) and a score of 4 for drowsy-lively (Y-axis), the intersection will be inserted and counted in a space in the fourth quadrant of the grid. Figure 4.2 shows how this score is inserted into the *Affect Grid* instrument.

After identifying the intersection between the horizontal and vertical axes in the grid, it is possible to classify the interaction carried out by this user into the other UX attributes, thus classifying the interaction as emotionally stressful or depressing, exciting or relaxing.

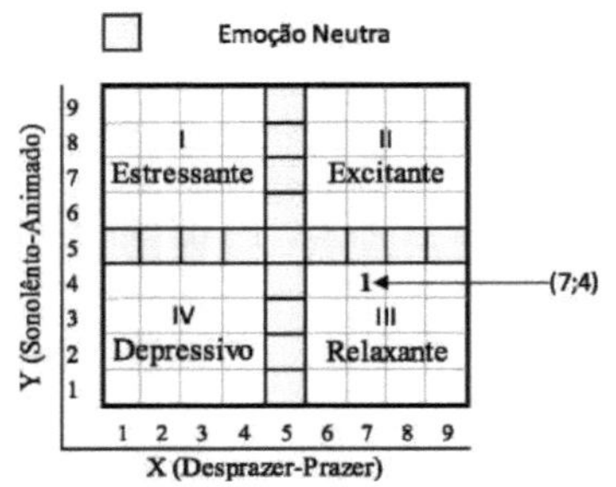

Figura 4.2: *Intersection of the X and Y axes of the Affect Grid.*

The Positive Affect and Negative Affect (PANAS) instrument consists of a questionnaire with 20 questions, 10 on positive affect (PA) and 10 on negative affect (NA), providing independent measures [21]. This instrument was developed in 1988 by researchers Watson, Wiese, Vaidya and Tellegen [100]. Since its inception, this measure has been used in research for various purposes. This popularity can be attributed to the fact that the instrument measures emotional effects during interactions with users, especially depressive emotions. Table 4.2 shows the positive and negative affect attributes of this instrument.

Table 4.2: *Attributes of positive affect and negative affect - PANAS.*

PANAS Questionnaire	
Positive Affect	**Negative Affect**
Interested	Angry
Lively	Anguished
Inspired	Embarrassed
Insurance	Upset
Determined	Nervous
Attentive	Guilty
Enthusiastic	Scared
Dynamic	Hostile
Proud	Tense

State of Alert	Frightened

Therefore, PANAS was used to investigate users' positive and negative affect after performing a set of tasks on a given website, while the *Affect Grid* analysed the emotions felt by users during the tasks. The two instruments complement each other in order to achieve the objectives of this research, thus assessing the emotional impact between blind and sighted users in interactions on responsive and non-responsive websites.

4.3.3 Usability questionnaires

In this case study, the usability questionnaires used were based on the following models: USE Questionnaire[4] , *Nielsen's Attributes of Usability* (NAU)[5] and *Computer System Usability* Questionnaire (CSUQ)[6] .The USE Questionnaire measures the usability attributes of applications in terms of usefulness, satisfaction and ease of use. Table 4.3 shows the usability attributes of the USE Questionnaire.

Table 4.3: *Usability attributes of the USE Questionnaire.*

Questionnaire USE	
Attribute	**Aspects**
Utility	That's more effective.
	That's more productive.
	That's useful.
	This gives me more control over my activities.
	This makes things easier to do.
	It saves me time.
	It meets my needs.
Ease of use	This is easy to use.
	This is simple to use.
	It takes fewer steps to achieve what I want.
	That's flexible.
	I can use it without help.
	There is no inconsistency in its use.
	I can easily correct navigation errors.
Satisfaction	I'm happy to use it.
	I would recommend it to a friend.
	It's fun to use.
	This works as expected.
	It's marvellous to wear it.
	I feel the need to use it.
	It's nice to wear.

The NAU questionnaire measures apprehensibility, efficiency, memorability, error accuracy and subjective user satisfaction [66]. Unlike the NAU questionnaire, the CSUQ questionnaire addresses both the overall system level and specific evaluation scenarios [52]. According to Lewis (1995), usability professionals can use this questionnaire to measure user satisfaction in interactions with systems in scenario-based usability studies [52],

Thus, the usability questionnaire used in this case study is an adapted combination of these three questionnaires. Table 4.4 shows the number of questions and the models that were followed. The full usability questionnaire is available in Appendix F.

[4]http://garyperlman.com/quest/quest.cgi?form=USE
[5]http://garyperlman.com/quest/quest.cgi?form=NAU
[6]http://garyperlman.com/quest/quest.cgi?form=CSUQ

Table 4.4: *Distribution of usability questions.*

Usability Questionnaire (Appendix F)	
Model	**Questions**
Questionnaire *USE*	Questions 02 to 10
Nielsen's Attributes ofUsability (NAU)	Questions 11 to 15
Computer System Usability Questionnaire	Questions 16 to 25

4.3.4 Test procedures

The tests were carried out on site, in an environment prepared for carrying out the tasks proposed in subsection 4.3.1. The participants used a computer with internet access and the browser that suited them. Figure 4.3 shows a schematic of the environment used to administer the tests.

Figure 4.3: *Testing environment.*

The scheme is made up of the moderator, who stands next to the participant during the test section, carrying out the interviews and filling in the questionnaires, and the assessor/observer, who helps the participants during the tasks.

The following tools were used to carry out the tests:

- MyCam[7] - A tool used to record videos of users during interactions on websites;
- AutoScreenRecorder Pro[8] - A tool used to capture screenshots while performing tasks;
- Jaws[9] - Assistive tool that helps you carry out tasks on websites (only for blind users);
- Hardware - Dell Vostro V14T-5470-A50 Ultrathin Notebook, Intel Core i7 Processor, 8GB RAM, 500GB Hard Disk with Windows 8 operating system and WebCam. The equipment had all the tools installed and configured.

The tools were selected following standard usability testing criteria, which define that in user testing, tools can be used to record the interactions and screens of the systems [92]. The Assistive tool was selected because all the blind users in the sample had previous experience using it for various purposes.

During the tests, videos of the interactions and audio were recorded in order to extract information that could be useful in the analyses. The systematic observation technique was used to analyse the emotional impact, usability and performance and identify the necessary correlations between them. According to Lakatos and Marconi (2003), systematic observation "takes place under controlled conditions to fulfil pre-established purposes"[49]. For the authors, the rules should not be too rigid, as the objects and objectives of the research

[7]https://mycam.apportal.com.br/
[8]http://www. wisdom-soft.com/
[9]http://www.freedomscientific.com/

may be different.

4.3.5 Data Extraction

To extract the information, a total of 648 (six hundred and forty-eight) videos and 648 (six hundred and forty-eight) screenshots were analysed while performing the tasks on the websites (subsection 4.3.1). Each video represented a task carried out by the user. Table 4.5 shows the number of videos and screenshots taken during the interactions.

Table 4.5: *Number of videos extracted in the search.*

Users	Video Capture		Screen Capture	
	Quantity	Hours	Quantity	Hours
Blind	324	23:10:40	324	21:52:03
Seers	324	05:41:30	324	05:22:15
Total	648	28:52:10	648	27:14:18

The analyses were carried out carefully in order to identify the possible barriers faced by users during these interactions. The following aspects were analysed:

- Number of tasks completed by users;
- Task completion time;
- User drop-out time for tasks;
- Number of errors during the task;
- Tasks not completed.

To analyse the emotional impact and usability during the tasks proposed in subsection 4.3.1, the answers to the *Affect Grid* (Appendix D), *PANAS* (Appendix E) and Usability (Appendix F) questionnaires were extracted. Table 4.6 shows the number of responses extracted from these instruments.

Table 4.6: *Number of answers extracted from the survey.*

Extracted answers			
Affect Grid	PANAS	Usability	Total
1.296	2.160	2.916	6.372

4.4 Data Analysis Procedures

The analysis of the research data is the phase in which descriptive and analytical analyses are carried out, interpreting and analysing the data collected during the application of the UX tests. According to Prodanov and Freitas (2013), analyses must be carried out in order to meet the research objectives and to compare and contrast data in order to answer the research questions [76].

According to Lakatos and Marconi (2003), "procedural methods are often used together in order to obtain various approaches to the object of study" [49]. Thus, in this case study, statistical methods were used to analyse the quantitative and qualitative data. According to the authors, statistical methods make it possible to "obtain simple representations from complex sets and check whether these simplified verifications are related to each other. Thus, the statistical method means the reduction of sociological, political, economic etc. phenomena to quantitative terms and statistical manipulation, which makes it possible to prove the relationships between phenomena and to obtain generalisations about their nature, occurrence or significance"

[49].

The following subsections present the procedures for the analyses carried out in this case study.

4.4.1 Analysing the Survey Sample

To describe the variables identifying the profile of blind and sighted users, absolute and relative frequencies were used for the qualitative variables and the mean and standard deviation for the quantitative variables.

According to Castanheira (2012), "the absolute frequency is the number of times the same result occurs in the same survey", i.e. the frequency of numbers that are repeated in a given sample [19].The relative frequency aims to make the data more significant by making comparisons using percentage data. Percentage data is defined as the ratio between the absolute frequency and the number of observations collected during the survey [19].

4.4.2 Usability Analysis

In order to carry out comparisons of usability attributes between the groups of blind and sighted users, in responsive and non-responsive design in the website categories, the Chi- Square Test was used for nominal variables and the Mann-Whitney and Kruskal-Wallis Test [42] for ordinal variables. The Mann-Whitney test is used to compare median values between two groups in the sample. The Kruskal-Wallis Test has the same purpose as the Mann-Whitney Test, but is used to compare more than two groups in the sample.

4.4.3 Performance Analysis

Kaplan-Meier curves [23] were used to illustrate task completion times between the blind and sighted user groups in responsive and non-responsive design, and comparisons between them were made using the Log Rank Test [23].

In this sense, Kaplan-Meier curves are able to describe the time until the occurrence of a given event (x-axis) and the Log Rank Test is used to compare the averages of time until the occurrence of a given event.

4.4.4 Emotional Impact Analysis (UX)

In order to compare the emotions felt by blind and sighted users while performing the tasks, two instruments were analysed: the *Affect Grid* and the PANAS.

The *Affect Grid* instrument compared emotions between blind and sighted users in tasks on responsive and non-responsive websites in the education, e-commerce and entertainment categories. To make these comparisons, the Chi-square test was applied and, when necessary, Fisher's exact test [3].

In this sense, the Chi-Square test checks whether the frequency found in a sample deviates significantly from the expected frequency. Thus, using the test, it is possible to compare proportions between two or more groups from the sample seti [93]. Fisher's Exact test serves the same purpose as the Chi-Square test for cases in which there is at least one expected frequency lower than 5.

In order to compare the displeasure-pleasure and drowsy-lively attributes of the *Affect Grid,* correlating the groups of blind and sighted users in responsive and non-responsive design, it was necessary to use Log-Linear Marginal Regression [35]. The Regression Model is used when there are repeated measurements of the same individuals, in which the model accounts for and incorporates the correlation between them.

A Log-Linear Marginal Regression was used to compare the Positive Affect and Negative Affect (PANAS) felt by blind and sighted users after performing a set of tasks in responsive and non-responsive design. In order to work with indicators that represented the set of emotions instead of working with each emotion separately, the Principal Components method [58] was used. The purpose of this method is to group together variables that are similar to each other (correlated).

The indicators created to represent emotions collectively were compared between the groups of blind and sighted users in responsive and non-responsive design among the website categories by means of Linear Marginal Regressions [35].

Therefore, marginal models, also known as the GEE *(Gene- ralised Equations Estimating)* method [53], can be considered an extension of Generalised Linear Models [56], which allow the expected correlation between measurements taken on the same user to be incorporated. Marginal Regressions, due to their ease of interpretation and absence of distributional assumptions, have been preferred as an extension of Generalised Linear Models for dependent data [35].

4.4.5 Correlation between analyses

Spearman's correlation coefficient [83] was used to correlate the variables in the *Affect Grid,* PANAS and Usability questionnaires. The Spe- arman correlation is a coefficient used to measure the relationship between two quantitative and non-normal variables. In this correlation, the coefficient has values between -1 and 1, and values close to -1 indicate a strong negative correlation, and values close to 1 indicate a strong positive correlation, while values close to 0 indicate no correlation [83].

4.5 Final considerations

This chapter presents a case study on the user experience of new web trends, specifically responsive design and *flat design.* The case study proposes a comparative investigation between blind and sighted users during interactions in a set of pre-established tasks on websites in three categories: education, e-commerce and entertainment. For each category, two websites were selected, one responsive and one non-responsive. Thus, six websites were selected for the case study.

It can be seen that the websites selected here needed to achieve a minimum accessibility index for blind users to be able to carry out their tasks. Another important aspect for choosing websites for the research was that the accessibility indexes of the two websites in each category, one responsive and the other non-responsive, could not have a difference of more than 0.5 between them.

This chapter presents the methodological approaches that were used to carry out the case study, presenting the scenarios and tasks, the instruments and procedures for analysing the data collection. Statistical methods were used to carry out descriptive and analytical analyses, interpreting and analysing the data collected during the interactions of blind and sighted users with new trends on the Web. Chapter 5 shows the results and discussions of this case study.

CHAPTER 5

Results and Discussions

This chapter presents the results of the analyses and discussions of the case study proposed in Chapter 4. This chapter is organised as follows:

- Section 5.1 presents the results of the analyses of the sample of survey participants.
- Section 5.2 presents the results of the analyses of the answers to the usability questionnaire, comparing the usability variables between the groups of blind and sighted users in responsive and non-responsive designs.
- Section 5.3 presents the results of the analyses of the performance of the blind and sighted user groups during the tasks.
- Section 5.5 presents the results of the emotional impact. Subsection 5.5.1 shows the results of the analyses of the *Affect grid* instrument with the percentage of feelings of displeasure and pleasure, drowsiness and excitement during the tasks proposed in subsection 4.3.1 of Chapter 4. Subsection 5.5.2 shows the results of the analyses of the PANAS questionnaire.
- Section 5.6 presents the correlations between usability, performance and emotional impact, comparing responsive and non-responsive design between the blind and sighted user groups.
- Section 5.7 concludes the case study results.

5.1 Research participants

This survey involved 18 users. 50 per cent of the user sample was blind. Of those who were blind, two users had acquired blindness and seven had congenital blindness.

With regard to computer experience, specifically the length of time users had been using the computer, all the individuals said they had been using computers for more than four years. Table 5.1 describes the other attributes that were assessed when identifying the participants.

Table 5.1: *Description of the variables identifying the research participants.*

Variables		General		Blind		Seers	
Sex	Female	2	11,1%	2	22,2%	0	0,0%
	Male	16	88,9%	7	77,8%	9	100,0%
Age	Average (D.P)	32,7	(9,6)	33,6	(10,5)	31,6	(8,9)
Level of education	Greater than superior	6	33,3%	2	22,2%	4	44,4%
	Less than Superior	12	66,7%	7	77,8%	5	55,6%
Time since finishing school Time since joining the course	Average (D.P)	5,2	(4,5)	7,5	(5,5)	3,3	(2,2)
	Average (D.P)	8,8	(5,7)	11,5	(6,8)	6,0	(2,9)
Time in the profession	Between 1 and 2 years	2	11,1%	0	0,0%	2	22,2%
	Between 2 and 4 years	2	11,1%	1	11,1%	1	11,1%
	More than 4 years	11	61,1%	6	66,7%	5	55,6%
	Less than 1 year	3	16,7%	2	22,2%	1	11,1%
Where you use a computer	Home	5	27,8%	3	33,3%	2	22,2%
	Home, Work	4	22,2%	0	0,0%	4	44,4%
	Home, Work, School	6	33,3%	5	55,6%	1	11,1%
	Home, Work, School, Other	3	16,7%	1	11,1%	2	22,2%
Hours of computer use per week	Between 2 and 5 hours	3	16,7%	2	22,2%	1	11,1%
	Between 5 and 10 hours	7	38,9%	3	33,3%	4	44,4%
	More than 10 hours	8	44,4%	4	44,4%	4	44,4%

Involvement in a usability/accessibility project Participation in a usability test	No	14	77,8%	6	66,7%	8	88,9%
	Yes	4	22,2%	3	33,3%	1	11,1%
	No	15	83,3%	6	66,7%	9	100,0%
	Yes	3	16,7%	3	33,3%	0	0,0%

Table 5.1 shows that 88.9 per cent of the individuals were male. The average age of the participants was 32.7 years, with a standard deviation of 9.6. Regarding the users' involvement in any usability/accessibility project, around 77.8 per cent reported that they had never participated or been involved in usability/accessibility projects.

5.2 Usability

To compare the usability questions (Appendix F) between the groups of blind and sighted users in responsive and non-responsive design, the Chi-square test was used for nominal variables and the Mann-Whitney and Kruskal-Wallis test [42] for ordinal variables. Table 5.2 shows the comparisons of the usability questionnaire variables between responsive and non-responsive design.

Table 5.2 shows the comparisons of the usability questionnaire variables between the responsive and non-responsive designs. In this way, it can be seen that the variables loss of identity of the site, difficulty reading the content, difficulty identifying an element, identification with the language, difficulty navigating the site and use of a search tool showed no significant difference between responsive and non-responsive designs, i.e. user experiences were similar with both responsive and non-responsive designs.

Table 5.2: *Comparison of the usability questionnaire variables between responsive and non-responsive design.*

Variables		Responsive	Not Responsive	p-value
Loss of site identity	No	38 70,4%	38 70,4%	1.000[1]
	Yes	16 29,6%	16 29,6%	
Difficulty reading the content	No	38 70,4%	44 81,5%	0,177[1]
	Yes	16 29,6%	10 18,5%	
Difficulty identifying an element	No	37 68,5%	33 61,1%	0,42o[1]
	Yes	17 31,5%	21 38,9%	
Identification with language	No	9 16,7%	9 16,7%	1,00o[1]
	Yes	45 83,3%	45 83,3%	
Difficulty navigating the site	No	37 68,5%	34 63,0%	0,543[A]
	Yes	17 31,5%	20 37,0%	
Use of a search tool	No	35 64,8%	36 66,7%	0,839[1]
	Yes	19 35,2%	18 33,3%	
Ease of use of the site	Average (D.P.)	3,54(0,15)	3,56(0,84)	0,858[2]
Demand for effort	Average (D.P.)	2,48(0,14)	2,78(0,79)	0,165[2]
Organising information	Average (D.P.)	3,39(0,13)	3,33(0,89)	0,769[2]
Accessible information	Average (D.P.)	3,5(0,13)	3,48(0,93)	0,841[2]
Sufficient information	Average (D.P.)	3,43(0,14)	3,26(0,99)	0,369[2]
Screen layout	Average (D.P.)	3,52(0,13)	3,43(0,82)	0,338[2]
Naming links	Average (D.P.)	3,57(0,14)	3,59(0,74)	0,560[2]
Assimilation of information	Average (D.P.)	3,56(0,13)	3,61(0,66)	0,926[2]
Easy to remember	Average (D.P.)	3,52(0,13)	3,52(0,77)	0,730[2]
Satisfaction with task time	Average (D.P.)	3,35(0,17)	3,3(1,06)	0,535[2]
Carrying out the test	Average (D.P.)	3,67(0,14)	3,48(0,97)	0,237[2]
Sites designed to access Iª time	Average (D.P.)	3,22(0,15)	3,22(1,04)	0,977[2]
Shortcuts	Average (D.P.)	2,87(0,15)	2,7(0,9)	0,427[2]
Easy to correct errors	Average (D.P.)	3,67(0,13)	3,28(1,11)	0,083[2]
Difficulty finding information	Average (D.P.)	1,85(0,12)	1,8(0,74)	0,876[2]

The variables ease of use of the site, demand for effort, organisation of information, accessible information, sufficient information, layout of screens, naming of links, assimilation of information, ease of remembering, satisfaction with the time taken to complete tasks, completion of the test, sites designed for first-time access, shortcuts, ease of correcting errors and difficulty in finding the desired information showed no significant differences between responsive and non-responsive designs.

Table 5.3 shows the comparisons of the usability questionnaire variables between the blind and sighted user groups. We can see that the variables loss of identity of the site, difficulty reading the content, difficulty identifying an element, identification with the language and difficulty navigating the site showed a significant difference between the groups of blind and sighted users. The group of blind users showed a higher percentage of loss of site identity, difficulty reading the content, difficulty identifying some element, identification with the language and difficulty navigating the site. There was no significant difference between the blind and sighted user groups when it came to the use of a search tool.

Table 5.3: *Comparison of the usability questionnaire variables between blind and sighted users.*

Variables		Blind	Seers	p-value[3]
Loss of site identity	No	32 59,3%	44 81,5%	O,©!![1]
	Yes	22 40,7%	10 18,5%	
Difficulty reading the content	No	35 64,8%	47 87,0%	0,007[1]
	Yes	19 35,2%	7 13,0%	
Difficulty identifying an element	No	28 51,9%	42 77,8%	o.oos[1]
	Yes	26 48,1%	12 22,2%	
Identification with language	No	13 24,1%	5 9,3%	0,039[x]
	Yes	41 75,9%	49 90,7%	
Difficulty navigating the site	No	26 48,1%	45 83,3%	0,00o[1]
	Yes	28 51,9%	9 16,7%	
Use of a search tool	No	39 72,2%	32 59,3%	0,156[1]
	Yes	15 27,8%	22 40,7%	
Ease of use of the site	Average (D.P.)	3,30(0,92)	3,80(0,13)	0,007[2]
Demand for effort	Average (D.P.)	3,06(0,71)	3,06(0,71)	0,000[2]
Organising information	Average (D.P.)	3,19(0,91)	3,54(0,13)	0,052[2]
Accessible information	Average (D.P.)	3,30(0,98)	3,69(0,12)	0,043[2]
Sufficient information	Average (D.P.)	3,07(1,06)	3,61(0,12)	0,006[2]
Screen layout	Average (D.P.)	3,41(0,86)	3,54(0,12)	0,549[2]
Naming links	Average (D.P.)	3,48(0,91)	3,69(0,12)	0,264[2]
Assimilation of information	Average (D.P.)	3,43(0,77)	3,74(0,11)	0,027[2]
Easy to remember	Average (D.P.)	3,26(0,87)	3,78(0,10)	0,001[2]
Satisfaction with task time	Average (D.P.)	3,09(1,22)	3,56(0,14)	0,055[2]
Carrying out the test	Average (D.P.)	3,46(1,08)	3,69(0,13)	0,293[2]
Sites designed to access Iª time	Average (D.P.)	2,96(1,17)	3,48(0,13)	0,031[2]
Shortcuts	Average (D.P.)	2,70(0,96)	2,87(0,14)	0,396[2]
Easy to correct errors	Average (D.P.)	3,44(1,02)	3,50(0,14)	0,792[2]
Difficulty finding information	Average (D.P.)	2,07(0,84)	1,57(0,09)	0,001[2]

The variables ease of use of the site, demand for effort, accessible information, sufficient information, assimilation of information, ease of remembering, sites designed to be accessed for the first time and difficulty in finding the desired information showed a significant difference between the groups of blind and sighted users. The group of blind users showed a greater demand for effort and greater difficulty in finding the desired information. The group of sighted users, on the other hand, found it easier to use the site, agreed more with the statement that the information was accessible and sufficient, found it easier to assimilate the information and remember where things were and agreed more with the statement that the sites were designed for first-time users.

The variables information organisation, screen layout, link naming, satisfaction with task completion time, test performance, shortcuts and ease of error correction showed no significant differences between the blind and sighted user groups.

5.3 Performance

Kaplan-Meier curves [23] were used to illustrate task completion times between groups of blind and sighted users in responsive and non-responsive designs in the education, e-commerce and entertainment categories, and comparisons were made using the Log Rank test [23]. Table 5.4 shows the comparisons of task completion times between blind and sighted users in responsive and non-responsive web design.

Table 5.4: *Comparison of task completion times.*

Subgroups		Comparisons	Median	I.C. - 95%[4]	p-value
Education	Blind	Not responsive	1,88	[1,58;2,88]	0,005
		Responsive	4,35	[2.68;Inf]	
e-Commerce	Blind	Not responsive	1,58	[0,88;2,37]	0,000
		Responsive	4,90	[3,53;6,7]	
Entertainment	Blind	Not responsive	1,50	[1,17;2,05]	0,093
		Responsive	2,03	[1,72;2,63]	
Education	Seers	Not responsive	0,62	[0,38;0,93]	0,021
		Responsive	0,80	[0,5; 1,62]	
e-Commerce	Seers	Not responsive	0,18	[0,15;0,23]	0,147
		Responsive	0,30	[0,23;0,38]	
Entertainment	Seers	Not responsive	0,49	[0,42;0,65]	0,054
		Responsive	0,37	[0,32;0,58]	
Education	Responsive	Seers	0,80	[0,5; 1,62]	0,000
		Blind	4,35	[2.68;Inf]	
e-Commerce	Responsive	Seers	0,30	[0,23;0,38]	0,000
		Blind	4,90	[3,53;6,7]	
Entertainment	Responsive	Seers	0,37	[0,32;0,58]	0,000
		Blind	2,03	[1,72;2,63]	
Education	Not responsive	Seers	0,62	[0,38;0,93]	0,000
		Blind	1,88	[1,58;2,88]	
e-Commerce	Not responsive	Seers	0,18	[0,15;0,23]	0,000
		Blind	1,58	[0,88;2,37]	
Entertainment	Not responsive	Seers	0,49	[0,42;0,65]	0,000
		Blind	1,50	[1,17;2,05]	
Responsive	Blind	Education	4,35	[2.68;Inf]	0,610
		e-Commerce	4,90	[3,53;6,7]	
		Entertainment	2,03	[1,72;2,63]	0,000
Not responsive	Blind	Education	1,88	[1,58;2,88]	0,491
		e-Commerce	1,58	[0,88;2,37]	
		Entertainment	1,50	[1,17;2,05]	0,281
Responsive	Seers	Education	0,80	[0,5; 1,62]	0,000
		e-Commerce	0,30	[0,23;0,38]	
		Entertainment	0,37	[0,32;0,58]	0,081
Not responsive	Seers	Education	0,62	[0,38;0,93]	0,000
		e-Commerce	0,18	[0,15;0,23]	
		Entertainment	0,49	[0,42;0,65]	0,000

From the multiple comparisons made in table 5.4, it can be seen that the responsive designs had a **significantly higher** median task completion time **than the non-responsive** designs **in the e-Commerce-Blind, Education-Blind and Education-Sighted subgroups.**

In all the subgroups, the group of blind users had a significantly higher median time to complete the tasks than the group of sighted users.

In the Responsive-Blind subgroup, the entertainment category had a significantly lower median task completion time than the e-commerce category, while the opposite was true in the Non-Responsive-Seers subgroup. Furthermore, also in the Responsive-Blind subgroup, the median time for the entertainment category was significantly lower than for education. In the Non-Responsive-Blind subgroup, the median time for the entertainment category was significantly lower than for education. In the Responsive-Sighted and Non-Responsive-Sighted subgroups, the education category had a significantly higher median task completion time than the e-commerce category. Graph 5.1 shows the Kaplan-Meier curves for task completion times between blind and sighted users in responsive and non-responsive design.

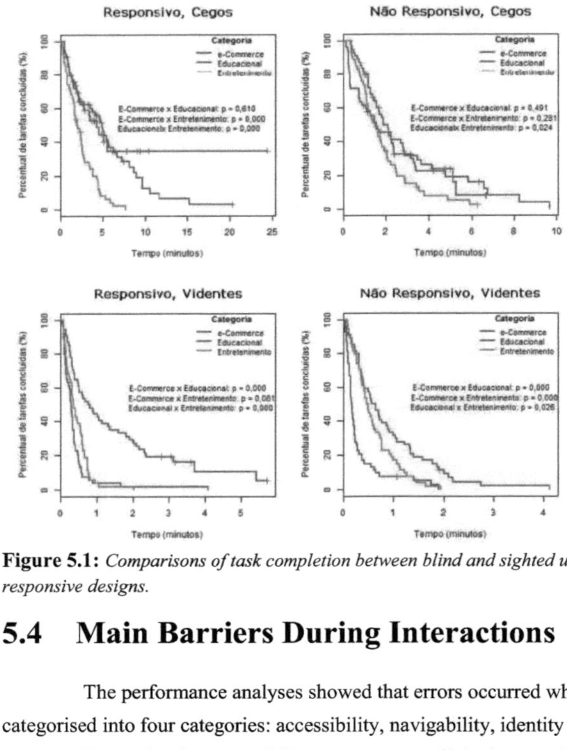

Figure 5.1: *Comparisons of task completion between blind and sighted users in responsive and non-responsive designs.*

5.4 Main Barriers During Interactions

The performance analyses showed that errors occurred when carrying out the tasks. The errors were categorised into four categories: accessibility, navigability, identity and content.

Errors in the accessibility category are linked to problems or barriers faced by users during interactions, caused by elements of websites that do not comply with the WCAG 2.0 accessibility guidelines. The other errors are problems or barriers faced by users during tasks that are linked to poor usability and lack of UX.

Table 5.5 shows the occurrence of errors/faults in each category identified during the tasks.

Table 5.5: *Number of errors that occurred during the tasks in responsive and non-responsive designs.*

Category	Group	Accessibility		Navigability	
		Blind	Seers	Blind	Seers
Education	Responsive	9	0	33	18

	Not Responsive	0	0	3	4
e-Commerce	Responsive	9	0	3	3
	Not Responsive	0	0	4	0
Entertainment	Responsive	0	0	**0**	0
	Not Responsive	9	0	6	1

Category	**Group**	**Identity**		**Contents**	
		Blind	Seers	Blind	Seers
Education	Responsive	0	0	2	8
	Not Responsive	0	0	**0**	0
e-Commerce	Responsive	0	0	**0**	0
	Not Responsive	0	0	**0**	0
Entertainment	Responsive	0	0	**0**	0
	Not Responsive	9	9	1	0

Eighteen (18) accessibility errors, seventy-five (75) navigability errors, eighteen (18) identity errors and eleven (11) content errors were identified. By identifying the possible barriers faced by users during interactions, it was possible to identify accessibility, navigability, identity and content problems.

- Accessibility problems:

- Twenty-seven (27) accessibility errors linked to priority 1 of the WCAG 2.0 accessibility guideline were identified during interactions in the Education-Responsive, e-Commerce-Responsive and Entertainment-Non-Responsive categories;
- In the Education-Responsive category, there were no *links* to bypass blocks of text. As a result, the assistive tool (Jaws) was unable to read the main submenus of the websites, thus increasing the time it took to complete the tasks. The menus also showed elements characteristic of Rich Web Applications (RWA) with inaccessible elements, making it impossible for the assistive tool to read them. This is because the assistive tool has difficulty reading elements of the *html* code, which are displayed and built at runtime;
- In the e-Commerce-Responsive and Entertainment-Non-Responsive categories, the absence of alternative texts on some images was noted. The existence of alternative texts for images allows information to be presented in various ways. The lack of content in the *alt* attribute makes it impossible to read using assistive tools, making the information inaccessible.

- Navigation problems:

- During the interactions, 75 (seventy-five) navigability errors were identified in the Education-Responsive, Education-Non-Responsive, e-Commerce-Responsive, e-Commerce-Non-Responsive and Entertainment-Non-Responsive categories. Observation showed that the vast majority of errors in the blind user group resulted from accessibility problems already reported in the previous topic.

- Identity issues:

- During the interactions, 18 (eighteen) identity errors were identified in the Entertainment-Non-Responsive category. These errors were caused by the fact that the website's search engine directs the search to *google,* thus losing the identity of the website, since blind and sighted users are directed to another website. A possible solution is to implement internal search engines with contextual information results to improve the usability and UX of these websites.

- Content issues:

- During the interactions, 11 (eleven) content errors were identified in the Education-Responsive and Entertainment-Non-Responsive categories. This error was caused by the lack of titles in the *layout* control blocks. It is recommended, in terms of both usability and accessibility, that the title of each section be described succinctly and clearly so that users can understand what the section of content will cover. The absence of these titles results in a longer average task completion time when compared to websites that follow usability and accessibility rules.

5.5 Emotional Impact (UX)

This section presents the results of analyses of the emotional impact of responsive and non-responsive design on the experience of blind and sighted users. To this end, the results of the *Affect Grid* and PANAS instruments are extracted and analysed.

5.5.1 Affect Grid

Using the *Affect Grid* instrument (Appendix D), it was possible to measure the emotional impact of users during interactions on websites in the emotional attributes of displeasure, pleasure, sleepy, excited, depressed, stressful, relaxing and exciting. The following subsections present the results of the extraction of these attributes.

5.5.1.1 Displeasure-Pleasure Scale

Table 5.6 shows the comparisons of feelings of displeasure between blind and sighted users in responsive and non-responsive design.

Table 5.6: *Comparison of feelings of displeasure and pleasure in Responsive and Non-Responsive Web Design.*

Category	Group	Design	Feelings			p-value
			Displeasure	Pleasure	Neutral	
Education	Blind	Not responsive	10 18,5%	29 53,7%	15 27,8%	0,064'
		Responsive	19 35,2%	18 33,3%	17 31,5%	
	Seers	Not responsive	3 5,6%	51 94,4%	0 0,0%	0,016²
		Responsive	6 11,1%	42 77,8%	6 11,1%	
e-Commerce	Blind	Not responsive	13 24,1%	35 64,8%	6 11,1%	0,245ˣ
		Responsive	16 29,6%	27 50,0%	11 20,4%	
	Seers	Not responsive	0 0,0%	53 98,1%	1 1,9%	1,000²
		Responsive	0 0,0%	54 100,0%	0 0,0%	
Entertainment	Blind	Not responsive	17 31,5%	31 57,4%	6 11,1%	0,0o!¹
		Responsive	2 3,7%	45 83,3%	7 13,0%	
	Seers	Not responsive	3 5,6%	49 90,7%	2 3,7%	0,237²
		Responsive	1 1,9%	53 98,1%	0 0,0%	

As table 5.6 shows, in the education category the group of blind users showed 35.2 per cent feelings of displeasure during the tasks carried out in responsive design. This percentage presented by this group of users was the highest compared to the feelings of displeasure presented by the group of blind users in the other categories, both in responsive and non-responsive design. Thus, in this same category, the group of blind users showed 53.7 per cent feelings of pleasure during tasks in the non-responsive design. Thus, in the group of blind users, the non-responsive design of the education category obtained a positive result when compared to the responsive design of the same category, but this result was not significant. In other words, the *p-value* was greater than 0.05. The group of sighted users obtained significant results in this same category, i.e. the *p-value* was less than 0.05, so that the group of sighted users showed 94.4% feelings of pleasure during the tasks in the non-responsive design when compared to the responsive design.

It can be seen that, in this category, the group of sighted users had a low percentage of feelings of displeasure during the tasks in both types of design, responsive and non-responsive.

Other categories that obtained significant results were the e-commerce category for the sighted user group and the entertainment category for the blind user group.

In the e-commerce category, the group of blind users showed 64.8 per cent feelings of pleasure during tasks in the non-responsive design and 50 per cent feelings of pleasure in the responsive design, but this percentage was not significant, while in the group of sighted users the results were similar in both the responsive and non-responsive designs *(valor-p=1.000)*.

In the entertainment category, the group of blind users showed 83.3 per cent feelings of pleasure during tasks in responsive design and 57.4 per cent feelings of pleasure in non-responsive design. This percentage was significant *(valor-p=0.001)*.

Therefore, there were significant results in the education category, in the group of sighted users, around 94 per cent of feelings of pleasure in responsive design, and in the entertainment category, in the group of blind users, around 83 per cent of feelings of pleasure in non-responsive design.

Analysing only the percentages of feelings of pleasure in the education, e-commerce and entertainment categories, the group of blind users showed higher percentages of feelings of pleasure in non-responsive design compared to responsive design. In the group of sighted users, the feelings of pleasure in responsive and non-responsive design were similar.

In order to compare the multiple emotions of the displeasure-pleasure scale between the groups of blind and sighted users, a Log-linear Marginal Regression was fitted. Tables 5.7, 5.8 and 5.9 show the results of the multiple comparisons for the displeasure-pleasure scale.

Tables 5.7, 5.8 and 5.9 show the multiple comparisons based on the fit of the Log-Linear Marginal Model for the Displeasure-Pleasure scale. In this way, we can

Table 5.7: *Multiple Comparisons for the Displeasure-Pleasure scale between responsive and non-responsive design - Log-Linean Marginal Model*

Subgroups		Comparisons	Doctor.	E.P?	Exp(P)[b]	I.C-95%	p-value
Education	Blind	Not responsive	5,96	0,28	0,81	[0,65;1]	0,046
		Responsive	4,82	0,31			
e-Commerce	Blind	Not responsive	5,91	0,30	0,92	[0,83;1,03]	0,134
		Responsive	5,44	0,30			
Entertainment	Blind	Not responsive	5,11	0,30	1,35	[1,18;1,55]	0,000
		Responsive	6,91	0,20			
Education	Seers	Not responsive	7,93	0,19	0,88	[0,77;1,01]	0,071
		Responsive	7,00	0,29			
e-Commerce	Seers	Not responsive	8,50	0,11	1,02	[0,99; 1,06]	0,209

		Responsive	8,69	0,09			
Entertainment	Seers	Not responsive	7,65	0,23	1,10	[1,01;1,2]	0,036
		Responsive	8,39	0,13			

Table 5.8: *Multiple comparisons for the Displeasure-Pleasure scale between blind and sighted users - Log-Linean Marginal Model*

Subgroups		Comparisons	Doctor.	E.P.	Exp(P)	I.C-95%	p-value
Education	Responsive	Seers	7,00	0,29	0,69	[0,57;0,83]	0,000
		Blind	4,82	0,31			
e-Commerce	Responsive	Seers	8,69	0,09	0,63	[0,56;0,7]	0,000
		Blind	5,44	0,30			
Entertainment	Responsive	Seers	8,39	0,13	0,82	[0,74;0,92]	0,000
		Blind	6,91	0,20			
Education	Not responsive	Seers	7,93	0,19	0,75	[0,63;0,9]	0,002
		Blind	5,96	0,28			
e-Commerce	Not responsive	Seers	8,50	0,11	0,69	[0,62;0,78]	0,000
		Blind	5,91	0,30			
Entertainment	Not responsive	Seers	7,65	0,23	0,67	[0,55;0,82]	0,000
		Blind	5,11	0,30			

Table 5.9: *Multiple comparisons for the Displeasure-Pleasure scale between the education, e-commerce and entertainment categories - Log-Linear Marginal Model.*

Subgroups		Comparisons	Doctor.	E.P.	Exp(p)	I.C-95%	p-value
Responsive	Blind	Education	4,82	0,31	0,88	[0,75;1,05]	0,160
		e-Commerce	5,44	0,30			
		Entertainment	6,91	0,20	1,27	[1,16;1,39]	0,000
Not responsive	Blind	Education	5,96	0,28	1,01	[0,83; 1,22]	0,923
		e-Commerce	5,91	0,30			
		Entertainment	5,11	0,30	0,87	[0,71; 1,05]	0,149
Responsive	Seers	Education	7,00	0,29	0,81	[0,73 ;0,89]	0,000
		e-Commerce	8,69	0,09			
		Entertainment	8,39	0,13	0,97	[0,92; 1,02]	0,171
Not responsive	Seers	Education	7,93	0,19	0,93	[0,88;0,98]	0,011
		e-Commerce	8,50	0,11			
		Entertainment	7,65	0,23	0,90	[0,83 ;0,98]	0,011

It can be seen that in the e-commerce category, in responsive design, the average on the pleasure scale in the group of blind users decreased by 37 per cent when compared to the group of sighted users. This difference was significant *(p-value=0.000).* In all groups, blind users had a significantly lower average value on the pleasure scale when compared to sighted users. The biggest difference between blind and sighted users occurred when analysing the responsive design of the e-commerce category and the smallest difference in the responsive design of the entertainment category.

In the education category, in the group of blind users, the average on the responsive design pleasure scale decreased by 19 per cent when compared to the responsive one. This difference was significant *(p-value=0.046).* In the Entertainment-blind and Entertainment-seeing subgroups, responsive design had a significantly higher mean value on the pleasure scale when compared to non-responsive design. In the e-Commerce-Blind, e-Commerce-Visidents and Education-Visidents subgroups, there was no significant difference between responsive and non-responsive design.

The Entertainment category, when compared to the e-commerce category, had a significantly higher mean value on the pleasure scale in the Responsive-Blind subgroup *(p-value=0.000)* and a lower mean value in the Non-Responsive-Seers subgroup *(p-value=0.011).* The entertainment category, when compared to the education category, had a significantly higher average value on the pleasure scale in the Responsive-Blind *(p-value=0.000)* and Responsive-Seers *(p-value=0.003)* subgroups. On the other hand, the education category, when compared to the e-commerce category, had a significantly lower average value in the Responsive-Seers *(p-value=0.000)* and Non-Responsive-Seers *(p-value=0.011)* subgroups.

5.5.1.2 Drowsy-Anxious Scale

Table 5.10 shows the comparisons of drowsy and excited feelings between blind and sighted users in responsive and non-responsive design.

It can be seen that in all categories the blind and sighted user groups had higher percentages of feelings of drowsiness than animation during the tasks in both responsive and non-responsive design. Analysing the percentages of the sample in the education category, the group of blind users showed a higher percentage of drowsy feelings in non-responsive design when compared to responsive design, but the percentages of neutral feelings were similar for responsive and non-responsive design. It was also found that feelings of animation were lower than neutral feelings, but the result in this category for the blind user group was significant *(valor-p=0.045)*.

In the entertainment category, the group of blind users showed 79.6 per cent feelings of drowsiness in the responsive design, while in the non-responsive design there were 46.3 per cent. It was also noted that the percentage of neutral feelings was higher than the percentage of animated feelings. This difference was significant *(valor-p=0.000)*.

Table 5.10: *Comparison of drowsy and excited feelings in responsive and non-responsive design.*

Category	Group	Design	Feelings			p-value
			Sleepy	Lively	Neutral	
Education	Blind	Not responsive	30 55,6%	3 5,6%	21 38,9%	0,045[1]
		Responsive	21 38,9%	11 20,4%	22 40,7%	
	Seers	Not responsive	53 98,1%	0 0,0%	1 1,9%	1,00o[2]
		Responsive	53 98,1%	0 0,0%	1 1,9%	
e-Commerce	Blind	Not responsive	32 59,3%	13 24,1%	9 16,7%	0,496[1]
		Responsive	29 53,7%	11 20,4%	14 25,9%	
	Seers	Not responsive	49 90,7%	4 7,4%	1 1,9%	0,372[2]
		Responsive	44 81,5%	7 13,0%	3 5,6%	
Entertainment	Blind	Not responsive	25 46,3%	11 20,4%	18 33,3%	0,00o[1]
		Responsive	43 79,6%	0 0,0%	11 20,4%	
	Seers	Not responsive	47 87,0%	5 9,3%	2 3,7%	0,034[2]
		Responsive	53 98,1%	0 0,0%	1 1,9%	

In the group of sighted users, feelings of sleepiness during tasks in responsive and non-responsive design were similar and the percentage in responsive design was slightly higher compared to non-responsive design. This difference was significant *(valor- p=0.034)*.

To compare the multiple emotions of the sleepy-anxious scale between blind and sighted users, a Log-linear Marginal Regression was fitted. Tables 5.11, 5.12 and 5.13 show the results of the multiple comparisons for the sleepy-anxious scale.

Table 5.11: Multiple comparisons for the Sleepy-Anxious scale between responsive and non-responsive design - Log-Linear Marginal Model

Subgroups		Comparisons	Average	E.P.	Exp(P)	I.C.-95%	p-value
Education	Blind	Not responsive	6,33	0,25	0,90	[0,8;1,01]	0,074
		Responsive	5,70	0,29			
e-Commerce	Blind	Not responsive	6,28	0,28	0,94	[0,84; 1,06]	0,342
		Responsive	5,93	0,29			
Entertainment	Blind	Not responsive	5,72	0,30	1,23	[1,08;1,4]	0,002
		Responsive	7,02	0,21			
Education	Seers	Not responsive	7,80	0,24	0,93	[0,83; 1,04]	0,212

		Responsive	7,26	0,28			
e-Commerce	Seers	Not responsive	8,44	0,12	1,01	[0,98;1,05]	0,496
		Responsive	8,56	0,11			
Entertainment	Seers	Not responsive	7,44	0,26	1,10	[0,98;1,23]	0,101
		Responsive	8,17	0,13			

Tables 5.11, 5.12 and 5.13 show the multiple comparisons based on the fit of the log-linear marginal model for the Drowsy-Animated scale. In this way, it can be seen that in the entertainment category, in the group of blind users, the average on the animation scale in responsive design increased by 23 per cent when compared to the non-blind group.

Table 5.12: *Multiple comparisons for the Sleepy-Animate scale between blind and sighted users - Log-Linear Marginal Model.*

Subgroups		Comparisons	Average	E.P.	Exp(P)	I.C.-95%	p-value
Education	Responsive	Seers	7,26	0,28	0,79	[0,67;0,93]	0,004
		Blind	5,70	0,29			
e-Commerce	Responsive	Seers	8,56	0,11	0,69	[0,61 ;0,78]	0,000
		Blind	5,93	0,29			
Entertainment	Responsive	Seers	8,17	0,13	0,86	[0,76;0,97]	0,017
		Blind	7,02	0,21			
Education	Not responsive	Seers	7,80	0,24	0,81	[0,69;0,95]	0,010
		Blind	6,33	0,25			
e-Commerce	Not responsive	Seers	8,44	0,12	0,74	[0,64;0,87]	0,000
		Blind	6,28	0,28			
Entertainment	Not responsive	Seers	7,44	0,26	0,77	[0,61 ;0,97]	0,026
		Blind	5,72	0,30			

Table 5.13: *Multiple comparisons for the Sleepy-Anxious scale between the education, e-commerce and entertainment categories - Log-Linear Marginal Model.*

Subgroups		Comparisons	Average	E.P.	Exp(P)	I.C.-95%	p-value
Responsive	Blind	Education	5,70	0,29	0,96	[0,88;1,06]	0,426
		e-Commerce	5,93	0,29			
		Entertainment	7,02	0,21	1,18	[1,07;1,32]	0,002
Not responsive	Blind	Education	6,33	0,25	1,01	[0,82; 1,24]	0,933
		e-Commerce	6,28	0,28			
		Entertainment	5,72	0,30	0,91	[0,73; 1,15]	0,426
Responsive	Seers	Education	7,26	0,28	0,85	[0,77;0,93]	0,001
		e-Commerce	8,56	0,11			
		Entertainment	8,17	0,13	0,95	[0,91;1]	0,076
Not responsive	Seers	Education	7,80	0,24	0,92	[0,85;1]	0,048
		e-Commerce	8,44	0,12			
		Entertainment	7,44	0,26	0,88	[0,8;0,97]	0,012

responsive. This difference was significant *(p-value=0.002)*. The other subgroups showed no significant difference between responsive and non-responsive design.

In the e-commerce category, in responsive design, the average on the animation scale in the group of blind users decreased by 31 per cent when compared to the group of sighted users. This difference was significant *(p-value=0.000)*. In all the subgroups, blind users had a significantly lower average value on the animation scale when compared to sighted users, and the biggest difference between blind and sighted users occurred when analysing the e-Commerce-Responsive subgroup and the smallest difference in the Entertainment-Responsive subgroup.

The entertainment category, when compared to the e-commerce category, had a significantly higher mean value on the animation scale in the Responsive-Blind subgroup *(p-value = 0.002)* and a lower mean value in the Non-Responsive-Sighted subgroup *(p-value = 0.012)*. The entertainment category, when compared to the education category, had a significantly lower average value on the animation scale in the Responsive-Blind subgroup *(p-value=0.002)* and a higher average value in the Responsive-Seers subgroup *(p-value=0.048)*. On the other hand, the education category, when compared to the e-commerce category, had a significantly lower average value in the Responsive-Seers *(p-value=0.001)* and Non-Responsive-Seers *(Va-lorp=0.048)* subgroups.

5.5.1.3 Depressive-Stressful and Relaxing-Exciting Scale

This subsection presents the extractions and comparisons of the other feelings felt by users when carrying out tasks in responsive and non-responsive design. For a better analysis, the results of this extraction have been divided into six tables, three for the extraction of depressive-stressful feelings and three for the extraction of drowsy-animated feelings.

Table 5.14: *Comparison of depressive and stressful feelings between responsive and non-responsive design.*

Subgroups		Comparisons	Feelings			p-value
			Depressed	Stressful	Neutral	
e-Commerce	Blind	Not Responsive	11 20,4%	1 1,9%	11 20,4%	0,067²
		Responsive	7 13,0%	3 5,6%	19 35,2%	
Education	Blind	Not Responsive	2 3,7%	5 9,%	24 44,4%	0,277²
		Responsive	5 9,3%	8 14,8%	25 46,3%	
Entertainment	Blind	Not Responsive	9 16,7%	3 5,6%	18 33,3%	0,00o²
		Responsive	0 0,0%	0 0,0%	12 22,2%	
e-Commerce	Seers	Not Responsive	0 0,0%	0 0,0%	1 1,9%	hOOO²
		Responsive	0 0,0%	0 0,0%	1 1,9%	
Education	Seers	Not Responsive	3 5,6%	0 0,0%	1 1,9%	0,035²
		Responsive	4 7,4%	2 3,7%	8 14,8%	
Entertainment	Seers	Not Responsive	3 5,6%	0 0,0%	3 5,6%	0,145²
		Responsive	0 0,0%	0 0,0%	1 1,9%	

Table 5.15: Comparison of depressive and stressful feelings between blind and sighted users.

Subgroups		Comparisons	Feelings			p-value
			Depressed	Stressful	Neutral	
e-Commerce	Responsive	Seers	0 0,0%	0 0,0%	1 1,9%	0,000²
		Blind	7 13,0%	3 5,6%	19 35,2%	
Education	Responsive	Seers	4 7,4%	2 3,7%	8 14,8%	0,000²
		Blind	5 9,3%	8 14,8%	25 46,3%	
Entertainment	Responsive	Seers	0 0,0%	0 0,0%	1 1,9%	0,003!
		Blind	0 0,0%	0 0,0%	12 22,2%	
e-Commerce	Not responsive	Seers	0 0,0%	0 0,0%	1 1,9%	0,000²
		Blind	11 20,4%	1 1,9%	11 20,4%	
Education	Not responsive	Seers	3 5,6%	0 0,0%	1 1,9%	0,000²
		Blind	2 3,7%	5 9,3%	24 44,4%	
Entertainment	Not responsive	Seers	3 5,6%	0 0,0%	3 5,6%	0,000²
		Blind	9 16,7%	3 5,6%	18 33,3%	

Table 5.16: *Comparison of depressive and stressful feelings between the education, e-commerce and entertainment categories.*

Subgroups		Comparisons	Feelings			p-value
			Depressed	Stressful	Neutral	
Responsive	Blind	e-Commerce	7 13,0%	3 5,6%	19 35,2%	
		Education	5 9,3%	8 14,8%	25 46,3%	0,000²
		Entertainment	0 0,0%	0 0,0%	12 22,2%	
Not responsive	Blind	e-Commerce	11 20,4%	1 1,9%	11 20,4%	0,010²

		Education	2 3,7%	5 9,3%	24 44,4%	
		Entertainment	9 16,7%	3 5,6%	18 33,3%	
Responsive	Seers	e-Commerce	0 0,0%	0 0,0%	1 1,9%	
		Education	4 7,4%	2 3,7%	8 14,8%	0,000[2]
		Entertainment	0 0,0%	0 0,0%	1 1,9%	
Not responsive	Seers	e-Commerce	0 0,0%	0 0,0%	1 1,9%	
		Education	3 5,6%	0 0,0%	1 1,9%	0,352[2]
		Entertainment	3 5,6%	0 0,0%	3 5,6%	

Table 5.17: *Comparison of exciting and relaxing feelings between responsive and non-responsive design.*

Subgroups		Comparisons	Feelings			p-value
			Exciting	Relaxing	Neutral	
e-Commerce	Blind	Not Responsive	31 57,4%	0 0,0%	11 20,4%	0,067[2]
		Responsive	22 40,7%	3 5,6%	19 35,2%	
Education	Blind	Not Responsive	22 40,7%	1 1,9%	24 44,4%	0,277[2]
		Responsive	13 24,1%	3 5,6%	25 46,3%	
Entertainment	Blind	Not Responsive	22 40,7%	2 3,7%	18 33,3%	0,000[2]
		Responsive	42 77,8%	0 0,0%	12 22,2%	
e-Commerce	Seers	Not Responsive	53 98,1%	0 0,0%	1 1,9%	1,000[2]
		Responsive	53 98,1%	0 0,0%	1 1,9%	
Education	Seers	Not Responsive	49 90,7%	1 1,9%	1 1,9%	0,035[2]
		Responsive	39 72,2%	1 1,9%	8 14,8%	
Entertainment	Seers	Not Responsive	47 87,0%	1 1,9%	3 5,6%	0,145[2]
		Responsive	53 98,1%	0 0,0%	1 1,9%	

Table 5.18: *Comparison of exciting and relaxing feelings between blind and sighted users.*

Subgroups		Comparisons	Feelings			p-value
			Exciting	Relaxing	Neutral	
e-Commerce	Responsive	Seers	53 98,1%	0 0,0%	1 1,9%	0,000[2]
		Blind	22 40,7%	3 5,6%	19 35,2%	
Education	Responsive	Seers	39 72,2%	1 1,9%	8 14,8%	0,000[2]
		Blind	13 24,1%	3 5,6%	25 46,3%	
Entertainment	Responsive	Seers	53 98,1%	0 0,0%	1 1,9%	0,003*
		Blind	42 77,8%	0 0,0%	12 22,2%	
e-Commerce	Not responsive	Seers	53 98,1%	0 0,0%	1 1,9%	0,000[2]
		Blind	31 57,4%	0 0,0%	11 20,4%	
Education	Not responsive	Seers	49 90,7%	1 1,9%	1 1,9%	0,000[2]
		Blind	22 40,7%	1 1,9%	24 44,4%	
Entertainment	Not responsive	Seers	47 87,0%	1 1,9%	3 5,6%	0,000[2]
		Blind	22 40,7%	2 3,7%	18 33,3%	

Table 5.19: *Comparison of exciting and relaxing feelings between responsive and non-responsive design for the education, e-commerce and entertainment categories.*

Subgroups		Comparisons	Feelings			p-value
			Exciting	Relaxing	Neutral	
Responsive	Blind	e-Commerce	22 40,7%	3 5,6%	19 35,2%	
		Education	13 24,1%	3 5,6%	25 46,3%	0,000[2]
		Entertainment	42 77,8%	0 0,0%	12 22,2%	
Not responsive	Blind	e-Commerce	31 57,4%	0 0,0%	11 20,4%	
		Education	22 40,7%	1 1,9%	24 44,4%	0,010[2]
		Entertainment	22 40,7%	2 3,7%	18 33,3%	
Responsive	Seers	e-Commerce	53 98,1%	0 0,0%	1 1,9%	
		Education	39 72,2%	1 1,9%	8 14,8%	0,000[2]
		Entertainment	53 98,1%	0 0,0%	1 1,9%	
Not responsive	Seers	e-Commerce	53 98,1%	0 0,0%	1 1,9%	
		Education	49 90,7%	1 1,9%	1 1,9%	0,352[2]
		Entertainment	47 87,0%	1 1,9%	3 5,6%	

Tables 5.14, 5.15, 5.16, 5.17, 5.18 and 5.19 show that in the Entertainment-Blind subgroup, the responsive design had more exciting feelings compared to the non-responsive design, which in turn had more depressive feelings. In the Education-Visidents subgroup, the non-responsive design showed more exciting

feelings compared to the responsive one, which in turn showed more neutral feelings. There was no significant difference between responsive and non-responsive design in the other subgroups.

In all the subgroups, the group of sighted users had more exciting feelings compared to the blind. In the e-Commerce-Responsive and e-Commerce-Non-Responsive subgroups, the blind user group had more depressed and neutral feelings, while in the Entertainment-Responsive, Education-Non-Responsive and Entertainment-Non-Responsive subgroups, the blind user group had more neutral feelings. The same occurred in the Education-Responsive subgroup, but this still showed more stressful feelings in the blind user group.

It was noted that in all the subgroups, the education category had more neutral feelings compared to the others. In the Responsive-Blind and Responsive-Seers subgroups, the entertainment category showed more aroused feelings and, in the last subgroup, the e-commerce category also showed more aroused feelings. In the Non-Responsive-Blind subgroup, the e-commerce category had more depressive and exciting feelings compared to the others. The Non-Responsive-Visidents subgroup showed no significant difference between the categories.

5.5.2 Positive Affect and Negative Affect (PANAS)

After applying a set of tasks on a given website, the PANAS questionnaire (Appendix E) was applied. Using PANAS, it was possible to measure positive and negative emotions during these interactions. The variables representing emotions were compared between the types of design, responsive and non-responsive, in the blind and sighted user groups by means of a Marginal Log-Linear regression.

Table 5.20: *Multiple comparisons for sentiment - Log-Linear Marginal Model.*

Emotions	Groups	Comparisons	Positive Affect and Negative Affect				
			Average	E.P.	Exp(β)	I.C.-95%	p-value
Interested	Blind	Not Responsive	2,96	0,22			
		Responsive	3,07	0,24	1,04	[0,86;1,25]	0,700
	Seers	Not Responsive	3,00	0,26			
		Responsive	2,85	0,24	0,95	[0,83; 1,09]	0,471
Angry	Blind	Not Responsive	1,41	0,12			
		Responsive	1,56	0,16	1,11	[0,92;1,33]	0,280
	Seers	Not Responsive	1,19	0,09			
		Responsive	1,44	0,15	1,22	[1,06;1,41]	0,007
Anguished	Blind	Not Responsive	1,19	0,09			
		Responsive	1,26	0,11	1,06	[0,98;1,15]	0,118
	Seers	Not Responsive	1,19	0,09			
		Responsive	1,30	0,14	1,09	[0,91;1,31]	0,334
State of alert	Blind	Not Responsive	2,41	0,20			
		Responsive	2,56	0,20	1,06	[0,98;1,15]	0,136
	Seers	Not Responsive	1,96	0,15			
		Responsive	2,22	0,22	1,13	[0,98;1,31]	0,091
Lively	Blind	Not Responsive	2,67	0,19			
		Responsive	2,70	0,20	1,01	[0,87;1,18]	0,858
	Seers	Not Responsive	2,63	0,25			
		Responsive	2,82	0,26	1,07	[0,99;1,16]	0,100
Embarrassed	Blind	Not Responsive	1,15	0,09			
		Responsive	1,30	0,13	1,13	[0,85; 1,51]	0,410
	Seers	Not Responsive	1,07	0,05			
		Responsive	1,26	0,16	1,17	[1;1,37]	0,050
Upset	Blind	Not Responsive	1,11	0,08			
		Responsive	1,33	0,14	1,20	[1,06;1,35]	0,003
	Seers	Not Responsive	1,11	0,06			
		Responsive	1,26	0,13	1,13	[0,98;1,31]	0,091
Inspired	Blind	Not Responsive	2,44	0,21			
		Responsive	2,48	0,20	1,02	[0,85;1,21]	0,866

	Seers	Not Responsive	2,30	0,24			
		Responsive	2,41	0,22	1,05	[0,96;1,15]	0,320
Insurance	Blind	Not Responsive	2,70	0,21			
		Responsive	2,63	0,19	0,97	[0,81;1,17]	0,771
	Seers	Not Responsive	3,00	0,21			
		Responsive	3,15	0,20	1,05	[0,9;1,22]	0,538
Nervous	Blind	Not Responsive	1,30	0,14			
		Responsive	1,33	0,09	1,03	[0,83; 1,27]	0,796
	Seers	Not Responsive	1,19	0,09			
		Responsive	1,19	0,09	1,00	[0,92; 1,09]	1,000

Table 5.21: *Multiple comparisons for sentiment - Marginal Log-Linear Model.*

Emotions	Groups	Comparisons	Positive Affect and Negative Affect				
			Average	E.P.	Exp(β)	I.C.-95%	p-value
Guilty	Blind	Not Responsive	1,04	0,04			
		Responsive	1,07	0,05	1,04	[0.97;1,1]	0,283
	Seers	Not Responsive	1,19	0,11			
		Responsive	1,15	0,09	0,97	[0,82;1,14]	0,702
Determined	Blind	Not Responsive	2,93	0,21			
		Responsive	2,96	0,21	1,01	[0,92;1,12]	0,798
	Seers	Not Responsive	2,67	0,19			
		Responsive	2,96	0,24	1,11	[1,02;1,21]	0,020
Scared	Blind	Not Responsive	1,19	0,11			
		Responsive	1,44	0,13	1,22	[1,05;1,41]	0,007
	Seers	Not Responsive	1,30	0,17			
		Responsive	1,37	0,14	1,06	[0,85;1,32]	0,624
Attentive	Blind	Not Responsive	2,89	0,16			
		Responsive	2,85	0,21	0,99	[0.88;1,1]	0,819
	Seers	Not Responsive	2,96	0,20			
		Responsive	2,82	0,17	0,95	[0,81;1,12]	0,540
Hostile	Blind	Not Responsive	1,11	0,08			
		Responsive	1,19	0,09	1,07	[0,87;1,3]	0,524
	Seers	Not Responsive	1,30	0,15			
		Responsive	1,26	0,10	0,97	[0,76; 1,24]	0,817
Tense	Blind	Not Responsive	1,48	0,15			
		Responsive	1,63	0,17	1,10	[0,93;1,3]	0,263
	Seers	Not Responsive	1,37	0,14			
		Responsive	1,48	0,20	1,08	[0,84; 1,39]	0,547
Enthusiastic	Blind	Not Responsive	2,74	0,20			
		Responsive	2,82	0,20	1,03	[0,91;1,15]	0,655
	Seers	Not Responsive	2,44	0,22			
		Responsive	2,59	0,22	1,06	[0,98;1,14]	0,123
Dynamic	Blind	Not Responsive	2,63	0,19			
		Responsive	2,63	0,16	1,00	[0,9;1,12]	1,000
	Seers	Not Responsive	2,48	0,21			
		Responsive	2,85	0,19	1,15	[1,03;1,29]	0,017
Proud	Blind	Not Responsive	2,56	0,23			
		Responsive	2,63	0,25	1,03	[0,88;1,2]	0,711
	Seers	Not Responsive	2,56	0,25			
		Responsive	2,48	0,26	0,97	[0,89; 1,06]	0,515
Frightened	Blind	Not Responsive	1,11	0,08			
		Responsive	1,22	0,10	1,10	[0,97; 1,24]	0,128
	Seers	Not Responsive	1,07	0,07			
		Responsive	1,22	0,11	1,14	[0,91; 1,42]	0,248

Tables 5.20 and 5.21 show the multiple comparisons based on the adjustment of the Log-Linear Marginal Model. In the group of blind users, the average disruption in responsive designs increased by 20 per cent compared to non-responsive users. This difference was significant *(p-value=0.003)*. In the group of sighted users, the mean scores for irritation, shame, determination and dynamism were higher in responsive designs when compared to non-responsive designs.

The emotions interest, anguish, alertness, excitement, inspiration, security, nervousness, guilt, fright, attention, hostility, tension, enthusiasm, pride and fear showed no significant differences between the responsive and non-responsive designs in the blind and sighted user groups.Figure 5.2 shows the graphs with the results of the positive affect emotions shown in table 5.20.

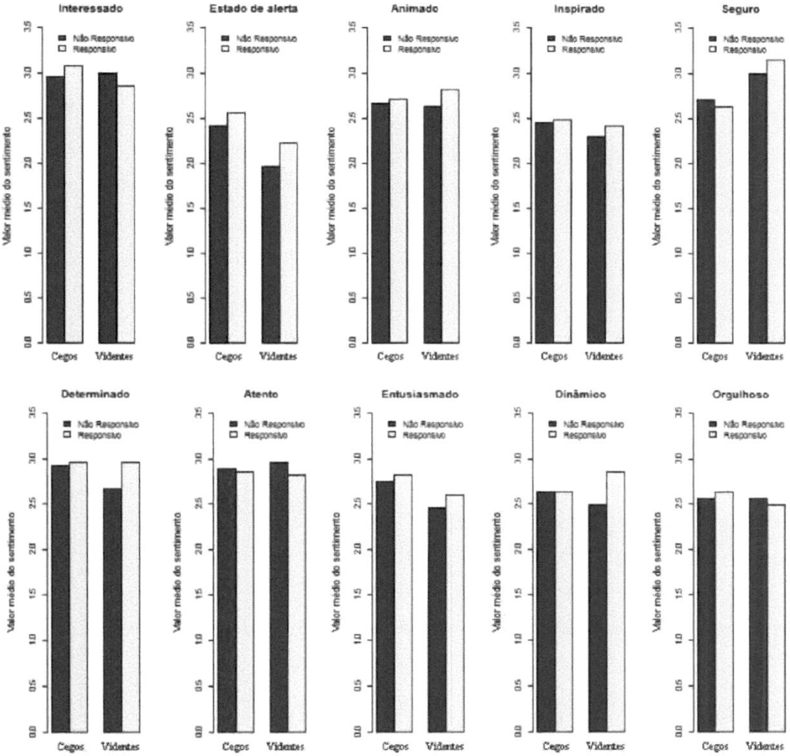

Figure 5.2: *Comparisons of positive affect emotions between blind and sighted users in responsive and non-responsive design.*

It was noted that in the positive emotions of interest, alertness, excitement, inspiration, determination, enthusiasm and pride, the group of blind users obtained higher results in responsive designs compared to non-responsive users. In the group of sighted users, the emotions of alertness, excitement, inspiration, security, determination, enthusiasm and dynamism obtained higher results in responsive designs compared to non-responsive ones.

In the positive emotions of interest, alertness, inspiration, enthusiasm and pride, the group of blind users obtained higher values than the group of sighted users in responsive designs. In non-responsive design, the positive emotions of alertness, excitement, inspiration, determination, enthusiasm and dynamism showed higher results in the group of blind users when compared to the group of sighted users.Figure 5.3 shows the graphs with the results of the negative affect emotions shown in table 5.20.

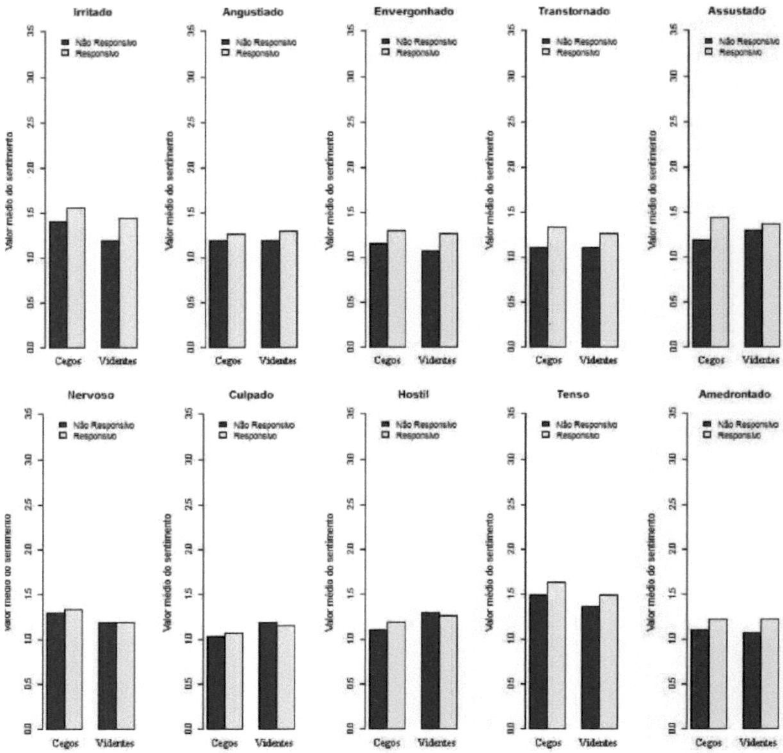

Figure 5.3: *Comparisons of negative affect emotions between blind and sighted users in responsive and non-responsive design.*

It was noted that, in terms of negative emotions, the group of blind users obtained higher results in responsive design compared to the non-responsive group. In the group of sighted users, the negative emotions of irritation, anguish, shame, upset, fright, tension and fear obtained higher results in responsive design compared to non-responsive users.

In the negative emotions of irritation, shame, upset, fright, nervousness, tension and fear, the group of blind users obtained higher values than the group of sighted users in responsive designs. In non-responsive design, the emotions of irritation, shame, nervousness, tension and fear showed higher results in the group of blind users when compared to the group of sighted users.

In order to work with indicators that represented the set of emotions, instead of working with each emotion separately, the Principal Components method [58] was used. Table 5.22 describes the weights of the principal components for positive affect and negative affect.

Table 5.22: *Weight of the Principal Components for Positive Affect and Negative Affect - PANAS.*

Variables	CP-1	CP-2
	(Negative-Positive Emotions)	(Intensity of Emotions)

Interested	0,240	0,212
Angry	-0,243	0,156
Anguished	-0,269	0,241
State of alert	-0,033	0,238
Lively	0,281	0,226
Embarrassed	-0,228	0,232
Upset	-0,248	0,231
Inspired	0,266	0,221
Insurance	0,243	0,118
Nervous	-0,146	0,227
Guilty	-0,132	0,111
Determined	0,191	0,296
Scared	-0,228	0,262
Attentive	0,156	0,221
Hostile	-0,218	0,184
Tense	-0,214	0,208
Enthusiastic	0,276	0,233
Dynamic	0,228	0,243
Proud	0,248	0,251
Frightened	-0,231	0,270
Variance Explained	30,9%	25,1%

The first two principal components were able to explain 56 per cent of all emotions and showed good interpretations. The first component (CP-1) was called the "Negative-Positive Emotions" scale, since, based on the weights shown in Table 5.22, the lower the scale, the higher the negative emotions (irritated, distressed, alert, ashamed, upset, nervous, scared, hostile, tense and afraid) and the lower the positive emotions (interested, excited, inspired, secure, determined, attentive, enthusiastic, dynamic and proud), while the higher the scale, the lower the negative emotions and the higher the positive emotions. The second component (CP-2) was called the "Intensity of Emotions" scale, since, based on the weights shown in table 5.22, the higher the scale, the higher the emotions, while the lower the scale, the lower the emotions.The "Negative-Positive Emotions" and "Intensity of Emotions" indicators (first and second components) can be understood as a weighted average of the emotions with the respective weights given in table 5.22. The indicators created are variables standardised by the mean and standard deviation, so they have a mean of zero and a standard deviation of one. Thus, positive values for the "Negative-Positive Emotions" indicator indicate that positive emotions are higher than negative emotions, while negative values indicate that positive emotions are lower than negative emotions. Positive values for the "Intensity of Emotions" indicator indicate that the evaluations of all emotions were above average, while negative values indicate that the evaluations of all emotions were below average.The indicators created to represent emotions collectively were compared between blind and sighted users, between responsive and non-responsive design types in the education, e-commerce and entertainment categories by means of Linear Marginal Regressions. Tables 5.23, 5.24 and 5.25 show the multiple comparisons for the "Negative-Positive Emotions" indicator using the Linear Marginal Model.

Table 5.23: *Multiple comparisons for the "Negative-Positive Emotions" indicator between responsive and non-responsive design - Linear Marginal Model.*

Subgroups		Comparisons	Average	E.P.	β	LC.-95%	p-value
Education	Blind	Not responsive	0,39	0,69	-1,76	[-3,45; -0,07]	0,042
		Responsive	-1,37	0,66			
e-Commerce	Blind	Not responsive	0,04	0,80	-0,87	[-2,99; 1,24]	0,420
		Responsive	-0,83	0,86			
Entertainment	Blind	Not responsive	0,12	0,70	1,39	[0,61; 2,17]	0,001
		Responsive	1,50	0,51			

Education	Seers	Not responsive	0,01	0,86	-2,23	[-5,36; 0,91]	0,164
		Responsive	-2,22	1,32			
e-Commerce	Seers	Not responsive	0,90	0,60	0,39	[-0,03; 0,82]	0,070
		Responsive	1,29	0,62			
Entertainment	Seers	Not responsive	-0,58	0,92	1,33	[-0,63; 3,29]	0,185
		Responsive	0,75	0,64			

Tables 5.23, 5.24 and 5.25 show the multiple comparisons based on the fit of the Linear Marginal Model for the "Negative-Positive Emotions" indicator. Thus, it can be seen that in the education category, in the group of blind users, the "Negative-Positive Emotions" indicator in responsive designs decreased by 1.76 when compared to non-responsive designs. This difference was significant *(p-value=0.042).* In the entertainment category, in the blind user group, the "Negative-Positive Emotions" indicator decreased by 1.76 when compared to the non-responsive group.

Table 5.24: *Multiple comparisons for the "Negative-Positive Emotions" indicator between blind and sighted users - Linear Marginal Model.*

Subgroups		Comparisons	Average	E.P.	β	I.C.-95%	p-value
Education	Responsive	Seers	-2,22	1,32	0,85	[-1,88; 3,58]	0,543
		Blind	-1,37	0,66			
e-Commerce	Responsive	Seers	1,29	0,62	-2,12	[-4,07; -0,17]	0,033
		Blind	-0,83	0,86			
Entertainment	Responsive	Seers	0,75	0,64	0,76	[-0,75; 2,27]	0,326
		Blind	1,50	0,51			
Education	Not responsive	Seers	0,01	0,86	0,38	[-1,66; 2,41]	0,718
		Blind	0,39	0,69			
e-Commerce	Not responsive	Seers	0,90	0,60	-0,86	[-2,71; 1,00]	0,365
		Blind	0,04	0,80			
Entertainment	Not responsive	Seers	-0,58	0,92	0,70	[-1,43; 2,83]	0,521
		Blind	0,12	0,70			

Table 5.25: *Multiple comparisons for the "Negative-Positive Emotions" indicator between the education, e-commerce and entertainment categories - Linear Marginal Model.*

Subgroups		Comparisons	Average	E.P.	β	I.C.-95%	p-value
Responsive	Blind	Education	-1,37	0,66	-0,54	[-2,39; 1,31]	0,568
		e-Commerce	-0,83	0,86			
		Entertainment	1,50	0,51	2,33	[0,80; 3,87]	0,003
Not responsive	Blind	Education	0,39	0,69	0,35	[-1,47; 2,16]	0,709
		e-Commerce	0,04	0,80			
		Entertainment	0,12	0,70	0,08	[-1,17; 1,32]	0,905
Responsive	Seers	Education	-2,22	1,32	-3,51	[-5,90; -1,12]	0,004
		e-Commerce	1,29	0,62			
		Entertainment	0,75	0,64	-0,54	[-1,39; 0,30]	0,208
Not responsive	Seers	Education	0,01	0,86	-0,88	[-2,04; 0,27]	0,132
		e-Commerce	0,90	0,60			
		Entertainment	-0,58	0,92	-1,48	[-3,25; 0,30]	0,103

Negative-Positive Emotions" in responsive designs increased by 1.39 when compared to non-responsive designs. This difference was significant *(p-value=0.001').* The other subgroups showed no significant difference between responsive and non-responsive designs.

In the e-commerce category, in responsive design, the "Negative-Positive Emotions" indicator in the group of blind users decreased by 2.12 when compared to the group of sighted users. This difference was significant *(p-value=0.033).* The other subgroups showed no significant difference between blind and sighted users.

In the Responsive-Blind subgroup, the "Negative-Positive Emotions" indicator in the entertainment category increased by 2.33 when compared to the e-commerce category *(p-value=0.003)*. In the Responsive-Blind and Responsive-Visual subgroups, the "Negative-Positive Emotions" indicator was higher in the entertainment category when compared to the education category *(p-value=0.000* and *0.042*, respectively). In the Responsive-Sighted subgroup, the indicator was lower in the education category when compared to the e-commerce category *(p-value=0.004)*.

Table 5.26: *Multiple Comparisons for the "Intensity of Emotions" indicator between responsive and non-responsive design - Linear Marginal Model.*

Subgroups		Comparisons	Average	E.P.	β	LC.-95%	p-value
Education	Blind	Not responsive	-0,91	0,60	0,75	[0,08;1,42]	0,028
		Responsive	-0,16	0,76			
e-Commerce	Blind	Not responsive	0,56	0,83	0,29	[-0,79;1,38]	0,599
		Responsive	0,85	0,67			
Entertainment	Blind	Not responsive	-0,10	0,69	0,60	[0,05;1,15]	0,031
		Responsive	0,51	0,65			
Education	Seers	Not responsive	0,19	0,84	1,57	[0,01 ;3,12]	0,048
		Responsive	1,76	1,09			
e-Commerce	Seers	Not responsive	-0,98	0,57	0,49	[0,08;0,91]	0,021
		Responsive	-0,48	0,57			
Entertainment	Seers	Not responsive	-0,52	0,77	-0,20	[-0,5;0,1]	0,184
		Responsive	-0,72	0,67			

Table 5.27: Multiple Comparisons for the "Intensity of Emotions" indicator between blind and sighted users - Linear Marginal Model.

Subgroups		Comparisons	Average	E.P.	β	LC.-95%	p-value
Education	Responsive	Seers	1,76	1,09	-1,92	[-4,37;0,53]	0,125
		Blind	-0,16	0,76			
e-Commerce	Responsive	Seers	-0,48	0,57	1,33	[-0,3;2,95]	0,109
		Blind	0,85	0,67			
Entertainment	Responsive	Seers	-0,72	0,67	1,23	[-0,49:2,96]	0,162
		Blind	0,51	0,65			
Education	Not responsive	Seers	0,19	0,84	-1,10	[-3,02:0,81]	0,260
		Blind	-0,91	0,60			
e-Commerce	Not responsive	Seers	-0,98	0,57	1,53	[-0,33:3,39]	0,107
		Blind	0,56	0,83			
Entertainment	Not responsive	Seers	-0,52	0,77	0,43	[-1,48:2,34]	0,660
		Blind	-0,10	0,69			

Tables 5.26, 5.27 and 5.28 show the multiple comparisons based on the fit of the Linear Marginal Model for the "Intensity of Emotions" indicator. It can be seen that in the education category, in the group of blind users, the "Intensity of Emotions" indicator in responsive designs increased by 0.75 when compared to non-responsive designs. This difference was significant *(p-value=0.028)*. In the entertainment category, in the group of blind users, the "Intensity of Emotions" indicator in responsive designs increased by 0.60 when compared to non-responsive designs. This difference was significant *(p-value=0.031)*. In the e-commerce and education categories, in the group of sighted users, the indicator was, respectively, lower and higher in responsive designs when compared to non-responsive designs.

Table 5.28: *Multiple Comparisons for the "Intensity of Emotions" indicator between the education, e-commerce and entertainment categories - Linear Marginal Model.*

Subgroups		Comparisons	Average	E.P.	β	LC.-95%	p-value
Responsive	Blind	Education	-0,16	0,76	-1,00	[-2,27;0,26]	0,121
		e-Commerce	0,85	0,67			
		Entertainment	0,51	0,65	-0,34	[-1,42;0,75]	0,542
Not responsive	Blind	Education	-0,91	0,60	-1,46	[-2,4;-0,52]	0,002
		e-Commerce	0,56	0,83			
		Entertainment	-0,10	0,69	-0,65	[-1,52;0,22]	0,145

Responsive	Seers	Education	1,76	1,09	2,24	[0,25;4,24]	0,027
		e-Commerce	-0,48	0,57			
		Entertainment	-0,72	0,67	-0,24	[-0,71:0,22]	0,307
Not responsive	Seers	Education	0,19	0,84	1,17	[0,17;2,17]	0,022
		e-Commerce	-0,98	0,57			
		Entertainment	-0,52	0,77	0,45	[-0,04;0,94]	0,070

In the Responsive-Visual subgroup, the "Intensity of Emotions" indicator in the entertainment category decreased by 2.72 when compared to the education category *(p-value=0.006).* The indicator was lower in the education category compared to the e-commerce category in the Non-Responsive-Blind subgroup *(p-value=0.002)* and higher in the Responsive-Seers *(p-value=0.027)* and Non-Responsive-Seers subgroups *(p-value=0.022).*

5.6 Correlation Between Usability, Performance and Emotional Impact

Spearman's correlation coefficient [46] was used to correlate the variables in the *Affect Grid,* PANAS and Usability questionnaires. The Spear- man coefficient, known as *r, is* a statistical measure that measures the intensity of the correlation between two variables. The correlation coefficient "r" varies between -1 and 1 and the closer it is to -1, the stronger the negative correlation, i.e. if one variable increases, the other tends to decrease. If the value is close to 1, the stronger the positive correlation, i.e. if one variable increases, the other tends to increase.

5.6.1 Correlation between Responsive and Non-Responsive Design

Table 5.29 shows the Spearman correlation coefficient between the variables in the *Affect Grid,* PANAS and Usability questionnaires in responsive and non-responsive designs. Significant correlations have been marked in bold. From the comparisons made in table 5.29, it can be seen that:

Table 5.29: *Spearman correlation between the variables in the responsive and non-responsive de- signs.*

Variables	Responsive			Not Responsive		
	T.T.	D.P.	S.A.	T.T.	D.P.	S.A.
(T.T.) Time Task	1	-	-	1	-	-
(D.P.) Displeasure-Pleasure	**-0,65**	1	-	**-0,56**	1	-
(S.A.) Sleepy-Animated	**-0,52**	**0,70**	1	**-0,51**	**0,80**	1
Interested	-0,02	**0,13**	**0,13**	-0,05	**0,28**	**0,43**
Angry	**0,18**	**-030**	**-0,20**	**0,24**	**-0,31**	**-039**
Anguished	**0,15**	**-0,25**	**-0,20**	0,06	**-0,16**	**-0,24**
State of alert	**0,27**	**-0,12**	-0,02	**0,11**	0,03	**0,12**
Lively	-0,03	**0,22**	**0,31**	0,05	**0,22**	**0,36**
Embarrassed	**0,19**	**-0,22**	**-0,16**	0,08	-0,10	**-0,11**
Upset	**0,15**	**-0,23**	**-0,17**	-0,01	-0,10	**-0,17**
Inspired	0,01	**0,25**	**0,32**	0,03	**0,16**	**0,18**
Insurance	**-0,27**	**0,32**	**0,39**	-0,08	**0,27**	**0,38**
Nervous	**0,23**	**-0,29**	**-0,26**	0,07	-0,04	-0,10
Guilty	**0,13**	**-0,23**	**-0,11**	-0,05	0,06	0,06
Determined	0,00	**0,19**	**0,23**	0,07	**0,12**	**0,14**
Scared	**0,18**	**-0,25**	**-0,21**	0,03	**-0,20**	**-0,28**
Attentive	-0,01	**0,17**	0,06	-0,04	**0,17**	**0,22**
Hostile	0,09	**-0,22**	**-0,11**	-0,02	**-0,11**	**-0,16**
Tense	**0,23**	**-0,28**	**-0,24**	0,08	**-0,14**	**-0,16**

Enthusiastic	0,03	**0,13**	**0,18**	0,06	**0,15**	**0,29**
Dynamic	**-0,15**	**0,21**	**0,33**	0,02	**0,20**	**0,33**
Proud	0,00	**0,17**	**0,13**	0,01	**0,18**	**0,30**
Frightened	**0,15**	**-0,22**	**-0,21**	0,06	**-0,14**	**-0,19**

- Regarding the time it takes to complete the tasks:

- In both the responsive and non-responsive designs, the higher the number on the Displeasure-Pleasure and Drowsy-Anxious scales, the shorter the time taken to complete the task, and the more irritated and alert the individual was, the longer the time taken to complete the task.
- Unlike the non-responsive designs, it was only found in the responsive designs that the more distressed, ashamed, upset, nervous, guilty, scared, tense and frightened the individual was, the longer they took to complete the task, and the more confident and dynamic the individual was, the shorter they took to complete the task.

- With regard to the Displeasure-Pleasure scale:

- In both responsive and non-responsive designs, the higher the number on the Drowsy-Anxious scale and the more interested, excited, inspired, secure, determined, attentive, enthusiastic, dynamic and proud the individual was, the higher their number on the Displeasure-Pleasure scale and the more irritated, distressed, frightened, hostile, tense and frightened the individual was, the lower their number on the Displeasure-Pleasure scale.
- Unlike the non-responsive designs, it was only found in the responsive designs that the more alert, ashamed, upset, nervous or guilty the individual was, the lower their number on the Displeasure-Pleasure scale.

- With regard to the Sleepy-Anxious scale:

- In both responsive and non-responsive designs, the more interested, excited, inspired, confident, determined, enthusiastic, dynamic and proud the individual was, the higher their number on the Sleepy-Anxious scale, and the more irritated, distressed, embarrassed, upset, scared, hostile, tense and afraid they were.
- Unlike the non-responsive designs, it was only found in the responsive designs that the more nervous and guilty the individual was, the lower their number on the Sleepy-Anxious scale.
- Unlike the responsive designs, it was only found in the non-responsive designs that the more alert and attentive the individual was, the higher their number on the Drowsy-Anxious scale.

5.6.2 Correlation between blind and sighted users

Tables 5.30 and 5.31 show the Spearman correlation coefficient between the variables in the questionnaires *Affect Grid,* PANAS and Usability between blind and sighted users. Significant correlations have been marked in bold.

From the comparisons made in tables 5.30 and 5.31, it can be seen that:

- Regarding the time it takes to complete the tasks:

- In both the blind and sighted user groups in the responsive and non-responsive designs, the higher the number on the Displeasure-Pleasure scale and the Drowsy-Anxious scale, the shorter the time taken to complete the task.

- In both the sighted user groups in the responsive designs and the blind user groups in the non-responsive designs, the more irritated the individual was, the longer it took them to complete the task.
- In the groups of sighted users, in both responsive and non-responsive designs, the more nervous the individual was, the longer it took them to complete the task.
- Unlike the others, it was only found in the groups of sighted users in the responsive designs that the more distressed, alert, ashamed, guilty, scared, hostile, tense and frightened the user was, the more they felt.

Table 5.30: *Spearman correlation between blind and sighted users of responsive design.*

Variables	Blind-Responsive			Seers-Responsive		
	T.T.	D.P.	S.A.	T.T.	D.P.	S.A.
(T.T.) Time Task	1	-	-	1	-	-
(D.P.) Displeasure-Pleasure	**-0,22**	1	-	**-0,54**	1	-
(S.A.) Sleepy-Animated	**-0,23**	**0,54**	1	**-0,35**	**0,73**	1
Interested	0,01	**0,19**	**0,18**	**-0,16**	**034**	**0,28**
Angry	0,02	**-0,26**	-0,11	**030**	**-0,34**	**-0,27**
Anguished	-0,06	**-0,15**	-0,14	**0,31**	**-0,41**	**-0,25**
State of alert	0,07	**0,24**	**0,30**	**0,25**	**-0,21**	-0,13
Lively	-0,09	**0,33**	**0,31**	0,03	**037**	**0,42**
Embarrassed	0,04	-0,06	-0,05	**031**	**-0,41**	**-0,16**
Upset	0,05	**-0,17**	-0,15	0,15	**-0,30**	-0,09
Inspired	0,05	**0,37**	**0,39**	-0,01	**035**	**0,33**
Insurance	-0,05	0,03	**0,21**	**-0,18**	**0,44**	**0,36**
Nervous	0,01	-0,12	-0,13	**031**	**-0,33**	**-0,16**
Guilty	0,08	**-0,17**	-0,02	**036**	**-0,41**	**-0,20**
Determined	-0,05	**0,24**	**0,23**	0,05	**030**	**0,33**
Scared	-0,07	-0,09	-0,13	**032**	**-0,39**	**-0,20**
Attentive	-0,05	**0,34**	**0,17**	-0,01	0,10	-0,01
Hostile	-0,04	**-0,25**	**-0,19**	**032**	**-0,35**	-0,09
Tense	0,00	-0,12	-0,05	**035**	**-0,33**	**-0,27**
Enthusiastic	-0,02	**0,18**	**0,22**	-0,06	**033**	**0,36**
Dynamic	-0,08	0,07	**0,26**	-0,04	**030**	0,26
Proud	-0,09	**0,20**	**0,20**	0,01	**035**	0,14
Frightened	-0,06	-0,08	-0,12	**037**	**-0,40**	**-0,23**

The more interested and confident the individual was, the shorter the time taken to complete the task.

- With regard to the Displeasure-Pleasure scale:

- In both the blind and sighted user groups in the responsive and non-responsive designs, the higher the number on the Sleepy-Anxious scale and the more interested, excited, inspired, determined, enthusiastic and proud the individual was, the higher their number on the Displeasure-Pleasure scale and the more irritated the individual was, the lower their number on the Displeasure-Pleasure scale.
- Both in the groups of blind users in the responsive and non-responsive designs and in the groups of sighted users in the non-responsive designs, the more attentive the individual was, the higher their number on the Displeasure-Pleasure scale.
- Both in the groups of sighted users in the responsive and non-responsive designs and in the groups of blind users in the non-responsive designs, the more secure and dynamic the individual was, the higher their number on the Displeasure-Pleasure scale.

Table 5.31: *Spearman correlation between blind and sighted users in non-responsive design.*

Variables	Blind-Not Responsive			Seers-Not Responsive		
	T.T.	D.P.	S.A.	T.T.	D.P.	S.A.
(T.T.) Time Task	1	-	-	1	-	-
(D.P.) Displeasure-Pleasure	**-0,23**	1	-	**-0,42**	1	-
(S.A.) Sleepy-Animated	**-0,28**	**0,65**	1	**-033**	**0,85**	1
Interested	-0,11	**030**	**0,47**	-0,02	**0,43**	**0,53**
Angry	**0,18**	**-0,18**	**-0,40**	0,13	**-0,27**	**-0,21**
Anguished	-0,01	-0,08	**-0,16**	0,14	**-0,31**	**-0,37**
State of alert	-0,06	**032**	**0,34**	0,07	0,11	**0,19**
Lively	0,03	**035**	**0,49**	0,05	**0,41**	**0,46**
Embarrassed	-0,01	0,02	-0,07	0,12	**-0,13**	-0,04
Upset	-0,08	0,07	0,02	0,15	**-0,34**	**-0,41**
Inspired	-0,08	**033**	**0,27**	0,04	**0,32**	**0,31**
Insurance	-0,10	**031**	**0,47**	0,08	**0,21**	**0,27**
Nervous	-0,12	0,11	-0,02	**0,22**	-0,14	-0,10
Guilty	-0,03	-0,08	-0,08	0,08	0,00	0,04
Determined	-0,06	**034**	**0,23**	0,04	**0,23**	**0,28**
Scared	0,01	-0,12	**-0,18**	0,11	**-0,34**	**-0,39**
Attentive	-0,06	**0,18**	**0,31**	0,06	**0,18**	0,15
Hostile	-0,04	-0,03	-0,11	0,14	**-0,33**	**-0,33**
Tense	-0,04	-0,12	**-0,27**	0,11	-0,13	0,04
Enthusiastic	-0,07	**037**	**0,43**	0,00	**0,40**	**0,46**
Dynamic	-0,12	**039**	**0,49**	0,07	**0,30**	**0,32**
Proud	-0,10	**030**	**0,51**	0,11	**0,21**	**0,25**
Frightened	-0,04	-0,03	-0,11	0,08	**-0,20**	**-0,22**

- Both in the groups of sighted users in the responsive and non-responsive designs and in the groups of blind users in the responsive designs, the more distressed, upset and hostile the individual was, the lower their number on the Displeasure-Pleasure scale.
- Both in the groups of blind users in the responsive and non-responsive designs and in the groups of sighted users in the responsive designs, the more alert the individual was, the higher their number on the Displeasure-Pleasure scale.
- In the responsive designs, in both the blind and sighted user groups, the more guilty the individual was, the lower their number on the Displeasure-Pleasure scale.
- In the groups of sighted users, in both responsive and non-responsive designs, the more embarrassed, scared and frightened the individual was, the lower their number on the Displeasure-Pleasure scale.

- With regard to the Sleepy-Anxious scale

- In both the blind and sighted user groups in the responsive and non-responsive designs, the more interested, excited, inspired, confident, determined and enthusiastic the individual was, the higher their number on the Sleepy-Anxious scale.
- Both in the group of blind users in the responsive and non-responsive designs and in the group of sighted users in the non-responsive designs, the more alert, dynamic and proud the individual was, the higher their number on the Sleepy-Anxious scale.
- Both in the group of sighted users in the responsive and non-responsive designs and in the group of blind users in the non-responsive designs, the more irritated, distressed and frightened the individual was, the lower their number on the Sleepy-Anxious scale.

- In the group of blind users, in both responsive and non-responsive designs, the more attentive the individual was, the higher their number on the Sleepy-Anxious scale.
- In both the group of blind users in the responsive designs and the group of sighted users in the non-responsive designs, the more hostile the individual was, the lower their number on the Sleepy-Anxious scale.
- In both the group of blind users in the non-responsive designs and the group of sighted users in the responsive designs, the more tense the individual was, the lower their number on the Sleepy-Anxious scale.
- In both the group of sighted users in the non-responsive designs and the group of sighted users in the responsive designs, the more frightened the individual was, the lower their number on the Sleepy-Anxious scale.
- Unlike the others, it was only in the group of blind users in the non-responsive designs that the more confident and determined the individual was, the higher their number on the Drowsy-Anxious scale.
- Unlike the others, it was only in the group of sighted users in the non-responsive designs that the more upset the individual was, the lower their number on the Drowsy-Anxious scale.
- Unlike the others, it was only found in the group of sighted users in the responsive designs that the more embarrassed, nervous and guilty the individual was, the lower their number on the Sleepy-Anxious scale.

5.7 Final considerations

5.7.1 Education Category

In the education category, in the group of blind users, non-responsive designs show more feelings of animation compared to responsive designs, which in turn show more feelings of drowsiness.

Regarding the indicators in the education category, in the group of blind users, the "Negative-Positive Emotions" indicator in responsive designs decreased by 1.76 when compared to non-responsive designs and the "Intensity of Emotions" indicator in responsive designs increased by 0.75 when compared to non-responsive designs.

In this same category, in the group of sighted users, non-responsive design showed more feelings of pleasure compared to responsive design. In this same group of users, non-responsive design presented more exciting feelings when compared to responsive design, which in turn presented more neutral feelings. Thus, considering these aspects, it can be concluded that the experience of blind and sighted users, in the education category, was better in the non-responsive design when compared to the responsive one. This result may be related to the large number of navigational errors or barriers that were identified during design interactions. Some of these barriers are related to the accessibility problems identified in subsection 5.4.

5.7.2 e-Commerce category

In the e-Commerce category, in the group of blind users, the average disruption in responsive design increased by 20 per cent when compared to non-responsive design. In this same category, in responsive design, the average on the pleasure scale in the blind user group decreased by 37 per cent when compared to the sighted user group.

In the group of sighted users, the averages for irritation, shame, determination and dynamism were higher in responsive designs than in non-responsive designs. With regard to the "Intensity of Emotions" indicator, in this same group of users, the indicator was lower in the responsive design when compared to the non-responsive design.

Thus, considering these aspects, it can be concluded that the experience of blind users in the e-Commerce category was better in the non-responsive design when compared to the responsive design. However, the experience of sighted users was better in the responsive design when compared to the non-responsive design.

5.7.3 Entertainment category

The statistical analyses led to the conclusion that in the entertainment category in the blind user group, responsive designs had more exciting feelings compared to non-responsive designs, which in turn had more depressive feelings. At the same time, in this same category, the non-responsive design identified possible errors when carrying out the tasks, which were classified as accessibility problems. In this same group of users, non-responsive designs showed more feelings of displeasure when compared to responsive designs.

With regard to the "Negative-Positive Emotions" and "Intensity of Emotions" indicators in the entertainment category, in the blind user group there was an increase of 1.39 in the "Negative-Positive Emotions" indicator in responsive design compared to non-responsive design, i.e. there was a higher index of positive feelings in responsive design compared to non-responsive design. The "Intensity of Emotions" indicator in responsive designs increased by 0.60 when compared to non-responsive designs.

Thus, considering these aspects, it can be concluded that the experience of blind users in the entertainment category was better in responsive design when compared to non-responsive design. This result is justified by the large number of barriers faced by blind users when carrying out tasks in the non-responsive design.

5.7.4 Other observations

The analyses show that responsive designs had a significantly higher median task completion time than non-responsive designs in the e-Commerce category for blind users and in the education category for blind and sighted users.

Another important aspect observed through the results of this research is that in all the subgroups, blind users had a significantly lower average value on the pleasure scale when compared to sighted users.

However, the biggest difference in user experience between blind and sighted people was found when analysing the responsive design of the e-Commerce category. The smallest difference, or similarity, in user experience was found in the responsive design of the entertainment category.

CHAPTER 6

Conclusion and future work

This chapter finalises the study, presenting its conclusion and future work. This chapter is organised as follows: section 6.1 presents the conclusion of the work and section 6.2 presents future work.

6.1 Conclusion

This section presents the conclusion of this work in relation to the research question raised in section 1.1 and the objectives proposed in section 1.3.

From the analyses carried out in this study, it can be concluded that blind and sighted users had a higher median task completion time in responsive designs when compared to non-responsive designs, and this difference was significant. With regard to the correlation between emotional impact among blind and sighted users, it was concluded that in the group of blind users, the average upset in responsive designs increased by 20% (twenty per cent) when compared to non-responsive designs. In the group of sighted users, this difference was not significant, but the mean scores for irritation, shame, determination and dynamism were higher in responsive designs when compared to non-responsive designs.

According to the results of the data collection, in all the subgroups that were compared using this approach, blind users had a significantly lower average value on the pleasure scale when compared to sighted users, with the UX of blind people being worse on responsive websites when compared to non-responsive websites. It was also found that in the groups of blind users, on both responsive and non-responsive websites, the more frightened the individual was, the lower their score on the Drowsy-Anxious scale and, unlike the others, it was only found in blind users on non-responsive websites that the more upset the individual was, the lower their score on the Drowsy-Anxious scale.

Thus, through the analyses, it was possible to verify the differences and similarities in the user experience of the new web trends between blind and sighted users, considering emotional and efficiency aspects.

It was therefore possible to measure the experience of blind and sighted users in these new Web design trends, and these results can be used to achieve greater levels of accessibility and acceptability by analysing users' emotions and feelings, thus acquiring, in addition to accessibility, a good user experience in the new Web design trends.

6.2 Future work

Based on this dissertation, the following future work could be proposed:

- Development of a UX framework capable of measuring the emotional impact of users during interactions with responsive and non-responsive websites by carrying out A/B tests;
- Make comparisons between the emotional impact and cognitive load of blind and sighted users when interacting with responsive websites;
- Measuring the experience of blind users in Rich Web Applications (RWA);
- Apply a comparative approach to a larger group of users, carrying out A/B tests on web applications for blind and sighted users;
- Developing applications that automatically monitor the emotional attributes of blind users, using image processing and computer vision.

Bibliographical references

[1] **Agile Manifesto,** 2001.

[2] ABES SOFFTWARE. **Brazilian Software Market - Panorama and Trends,** 2014.

[3] AGRESTI, A. **Categorical data analysis.** Wiley, New York, 2nd edn edition, 2002.

[4] ARAÚJO, A. F. D. **A Framework for Assessing the Level of Maturity in Software Testing for Micro and Small Companies.** 2013.

[5] BACH, C. F.; LEAL FERREIRA, S.; SILVEIRA, D. D.; NUNES, R. R. **Accessibility guidelines: a comparative approach between wcag and e-mag.** *SIMPÓSIO BRASILEIRO DE SISTEMAS DE INFORMAÇÃO, V,* p. 73-74, 2009.

[6] BADGETT, T.; SANDLER, C. **The art of software testing,** 2004.

[7] BECHER, A.; RODRIGUES, M. B. **Accessibility and Usability on the Web.** 2008.

[8] BIGHAM, J. P.; CAVENDER, A. C.; BRUDVIK, J. T.; WOBBROCK, J. O.; LANDER, R. E. **Webinsitu: a comparative analysis of blind and sighted browsing behaviour.** In: *Proceedings of the 9th International ACM SIGACCESS conference on Computers and accessibility,* p. 51-58. ACM, 2007.

[9] BONSANGUE, M. M.; CHAUDRON, M.; MERODE, H. V. **Integrating Testing into Agile Software Development Processes.** 2009.

[10] BOSE, R.; JÚRGENSEN, H. **Accessibility of e-commerce websites for vision- impaired persons.** In: *Computers Helping People with Special Needs,* p. 121-128. Springer, 2014.

[11] BRAGA, F. A. M. **An overview of the use of devops practices in the software industries.** 2015.

[12] BRAZIL. **Decree no. 5.296, of 2 December 2004.** Regulates Laws n. 10.048, of 8 November 2000, which gives priority service to the people it specifies, and 10.098, of 19 December 2000,

which establishes general rules and basic criteria for promoting accessibility for people with disabilities or reduced mobility, 2004.

[13] BRAZIL. **National Coordination for the Integration of People with Disabilities, Accessibility.** *Brasília: Special Secretariat for Human Rights,* 2008.

[14] BRAZIL. **Department of Electronic Government, Web Standards in Electronic Government: Usability Primer.** *Brasília: Secretariat of Logistics and Information Technology,* 2010.

[15] BROPHY, P.; CRAVEN, J. **Web accessibility.** *Library trends,* 55(4):950-972, 2007.

[16] CAMILO-JUNIOR, C. G.; VINCENZI, A. M. R.; RODRIGUES, C.; MARCOS, P.; LOU- ZADA, J.; BARBOSA, J. R.; DE ARAÚJO, A. F.; MARTINS, A.; SOARES, G. S.; PRUDENTE, M. J.; PESSONI, V. V. **FreeTest - Sofware Testing Process for Micro and Small Companies.** Website, Accessed August 2015. Available at http://www.freetest.net.br/downloads/Manualprocessoí-reeTesí.pd/.

[17] CAMILO-JUNIOR, C. G.; VINCENZI, A. M. R.; RODRIGUES, C.; MARCOS, R; LOUZADA, J.; BARBOSA, J. R.; DE ARAÚJO, A. F.; MARTINS, A.; SOARES, G. S.; PRUDENTE, M. J.; PESSONI, V. V. **FreeTest Method - web site.** Web page, Accessed August 2015. Available at http://www.freetest.net.br/.

[18] CARLO, J.; HAUCK, R.; SALVIANO, C. F. **Systematic Literature Review of Software Process Capability/Maturity Models.** (May), 2010.

[19] CASTANHEIRA, N. P. **Statistics Applied** AT **All Levels.** Curitiba: Ibpex, 5. ed. rev. and current edition, **2012.**

[20] CIRILLO, F. **The Pomodoro Technique**. 2010.

[21] CLARK, L. A.; WATSON, D. **Tripartite model of anxiety and depression: psychometric evidence and taxonomic implications.** *Journal of abnormal psychology,* 100(3):316, 1991.

[22] COHN, M. **Agile Estimating and Planning,** 2005.

[23] COLOSIMO, E. A.; GIOLO, S. R. **Applied Survival Analysis.** São Paulo: Edgard Bluche, 2006.

[24] CONSTANT, I. B. **Defining Blindness and Low Vision.** Website, Accessed August 2015. Available at http://www.ibc.gov.br/?itemid=94.

[25] FROM UFG, I. D. I. **Cercomp - UFG Computing Resources Centre.**

[26] DE, **E.**; DE, **N. Improving the Testing Process for Brazilian Micro and Small Companies. 2015.**

[27] DEBOIS, P. **Agile infrastructure and operations: How infra-gile are you?** *Proceedings - Agile 2008 Conference,* p. 202-207, 2008.

[28] DEGRANDIS, D. **Devops: A Software Revolution in the Making?** (August):1-8, 2011.

[29] DREHER, F. **Brazilian IT market expected to grow 2.6 per cent in 2016, says IDC.** Webpage,

Accessed August 2015. Available at http://cio.com.br/noticias/2016/01/28/mercado-brasileiro-de-ti-deve-crescer-2-6-em- 2016-afirma-idc/.

[30] DUVALL, B. P. M. **Continuous Delivery: Patterns and Antipatterns in the Software Lifecycle.** *CheatSheets,* 2014.

[31] ERICH, E; AMRIT, C.; DANEVA, M. **Report: DevOps Literature Review** (October), 2014.

[32] ESPECIALISTAS, I. D.; KIM, G. **DevOps: Hidden Risks and How to Achieve Results.** 2015.

[33] FERATI, M.; RAUFI, B.; KURTI, A.; VOGEL, B. **Accessibility requirements for blind and visually impaired in a regional context: An exploratory study.** In: *Usability and Accessibility Focused Requirements Engineering (UsARE), 2014 IEEE 2nd International Workshop on,* p. 13-16. IEEE, 2014.

[34] FITZGERALD, B.; STOL, K.-J. **Continuous software engineering and beyond: trends and challenges.** In: *Proceedings of the 1st International Workshop on Rapid Continuous Software Engineering - RCoSE2014*, p. 1-9, New York, New York, USA, 2014. ACM Press.

[35] FITZMAURICE, G. M.; LAIRD, N. M.; WARE, J. H. **Applied longitudinal analysis.** John Wiley & Sons, 2011.

[36] GIL, A. C. **Como elaborar projetos de pesquisa.** Atlas Editora, 5 edition, 2010.

[37] GOODHUE, D. **Altitudes: toward theoretical and definitional clarity.** 19(3-4):6-15, 1988.

[38] GOODWIN, N. C. **Functionality and usability.** *Communications of the ACM,* 30(3):229- 233, 1987.

[39] GROSS, S.; BARDZELL, J.; BARDZELL, S. **Skeu theevolution: skeuomorphs, style, and the material of tangible interactions.** In: *Proceedings of the 8th International Conference on Tangible, Embedded and Embodied Interaction,* p. 53-60. ACM, 2014.

[40] HAANPERÄ, T.; NIEMINEN, M. **Usability of web search interfaces for blind users-a review of digital academic library user interfaces.** In: *Universal Access in Human- Computer Interaction. Applications and Services for Quality of Life,* p. 321-330. Springer, 2013.

[41] HARTSON, R.; PYLA, P. S. **The UX Book: Process and guidelines for ensuring a quality user experience.** Elsevier, 2012.

[42] HOLLANDER, M.; WOLFE, D. A. **Solutions Manual to Accompany Nonparametric Statistical Methods.** Wiley, 1999.

[43] HOWLETT, S. **TestOps in a DevOps World,** p. 1-14.

[44] IBGE. **Brazilian Institute of Geography and Statistics, Demographic Census.** Brazil, 2010.

[45] JAAFAR, A.; YATIM, M.; OTHERS. **Astudy on web experience among visually impaired users in malaysia.** In: *2010 International Conference on User Science and Engineering (i-USEr),* p. 11-15, 2010.

[46] JAMES SHORE; SHANE WARDEN. **The Art of Agile Development.** volume 1, p. 1-121. 2007.

[47] JAMES WHITTAKER, JASON CAROLLO, J. HOW **Google Tests Software.** 2012.

[48] JÚNIOR; SALMO ROBERTO DA SILVA, D. F. P.; NET, S. C. **SCRUM: A Practical Guide to Project Management.** *Electronic Journal of Information Systems and Technology Management,* p. 1 - 17, 2015.

[49] LAKATOS, E. M.; MARCONI, M. D. A. **Fundamentals of Scientific Methodology.** São Paulo: Editora Atlas, 5 edition, 2003.

[50] LAPORTE, C. Y.; RENAULT, A.; ALEXANDRE, S. **The Development of International Standards for Very Small Enterprises History leading to an ISO / IEC Working Group for VSEs.** *International Organisation,* 2010.

[51] LAW, E. L.; HVANNBERG, E. T.; VERMEEREN, A. R; COCKTON, G.; JOKELA, T. **Workshop at the acm chi 2013 conference.** *ACM library,* 2013.

[52] LEWIS, J. R. **Ibm Computer usability satisfaction questionnaires: Psychometric eva- luation and instructions for use.** *International Journal of Human-Computer Interaction,* 7(1):57-78, 1995.

[53] LIANG, K.-Y.; ZEGER, S. L. **Longitudinal data analysis using generalised linear models.** *Biometrika,* **p. 13-22,1986.**

[54] MARCOTTE, E. **Responsive web design.** Webpage, Accessed October 2014. Available at http://alistapart.com/article/responsive-web-design/.

[55] MAULE, J. **Killer UX Design.** SitePoint: 1 edition, 2012.

[56] MCCULLAGH, P.; NELDER, J. A. **Generalised linear models,** volume 37. CRC press, 1989.

[57] MICHAILIDOU, E.; HARPER, S.; BECHHOFER, S. **Visual complexity and aesthetic perception of web pages.** In: *Proceedings of the 26th Annual ACM International Conference on Design of Communication,* SIGDOC '08, p. **215-224**, New York, NY, USA, 2008. ACM.

[58] MINGOTI, S. A. **Analysing data using multivariate statistical methods: an applied approach.** Editora UFMG, 2005.

[59] MITASIUNAS, A.; ROUT, T.; O'CONNOR, R. V.; DORLING, A. **Software Process Impro- vement and Capability Determination SPICE 2014).** 2014.

[60] MOHOROVICIC, S. **Implementing responsive web design for enhanced web presence.** In: *Information & Communication Technology Electronics & Microelectronics (MIPRO), 2013 36th International Convention on,* p. 1206-1210. IEEE, 2013.

[61] MOLINARI, L. **Software Testing. Producing Better and More Reliable Systems,** ed. são paulo edition, 2003.

[62] MUSTI, S.; KASHYAP, V. **Responsive Design: The Time is Now.** Vipro, 2013.

[63] NEIL, T. **Mobile Design Pattern Gallery: UI Patterns for Smartphone Apps.** O'Reilly Media, second edition, 2014.

[64] NICÁCIO, J. M. **Accessibility techniques: creating a web for everyone.** *Maceió: Edufal,* 2010.

[65] NIELSEN, J. HOW **Many Test Users in a Usability Study?** Webpage, Accessed August 2015. Available at http://www.nngroup.com/articles/how-many-test-users/.

[66] NIELSEN, J. **Usability engineering.** Elsevier, 1994.

[67] NIELSEN, J. **Why you only need to test with 5 users,** 2000.

[68] NIELSEN, J.; LORANGER, H. **Usability on the web: designing quality websites.** *Rio de Janeiro: Campus,* 2007.

[69] NINA, E. **KITest: A framework for knowledge and test process improvement.**

[70] PAN, Y.; BLEVIS, E. **Fashion thinking: lessons from fashion and sustainable interac- tion design, concepts and issues.** In: *Proceedings of the 2014 conference on Designing Interactive Systems,* p. 1005-1014. ACM, 2014.

[71] PASTORE, **S. Website development and web standards in the ubiquitous world: where are we going.** *WSEAS Transactions on Computers,* 11 (9), **2012.**

[72] PETERSON, **C. Learning Responsive Web Design: A Beginner's Guide.** "O'Reilly Media, Inc., 2014.

[73] PMBOK, G. **A guide to project management knowledge,** 2013.

[74] PRATAS, A. **Creating Fiat Design Websites: Design and develop your own flat design websites in HTML.** Packt Publishing, 2014.

[75] PRESSMAN, R. S. **Software Engineering: A Professional Approach.** São Paulo: Pearson Makron Books, 7 edition, 2011.

[76] PRODANOV, C. C.; FREITAS, E. C. **Metodologia do Trabalho Científico: Métodos** e **Técnicas da Pesquisa e do Trabalho Acadêmico.** Novo Hamburgo: Feevale, **2** edition, 2013.

[77] PUCILLO, F.; CASCINI, G. **A framework for user experience, needs and affordances.** *Design Studies,* 35(2): 160-179, 2014.

[78] RAFAEL, V.; MENDONÇA, L. D. **Study, Definition and Implementation of a Recommendation System to prioritise warnings generated by statistical analysis tools.** 2014.

[79] RAMACHANDRAM, S. **An evolutionary software product development process for small and médium enterprises (SMEs).** *2008 4th International Conference on Emerging Technologies,* p. 298-303, 2008.

[80] Rios, E. **Risk Analysis in Software Testing,** p. 1-12.

[81] RUSSELL, J. A.; WEISS, A.; MENDELSOHN, G. A. **Affect grid: a single-item scale of pleasure and arousal.** *Journal of personality and social psychology,* 57(3) :493,1989.

[82] SHAH, H.; HARROLD, M. J. **Culture and Testing: What is the Relationship?** 2013.

[83] SIEGAL, S.; JR, N. J. C. **Non-Parametric Statistics for the Behavioural Sciences.** Porto Alegre: Artmed, 2006.

[84] SOFTEX. **Model Reference Guide - MPT.Br.** Web page, Accessed in March 2017. Available at http://www.mpt.org.br/wp-content/uploads/2011/06/MPT(r)440.pd/.

[85] SOFTEX. **MPS.Br.**

[86] SPILLERS, F. **Emotion as a cognitive artifact and the design implications for products that are perceived as pleasurable.** *Experience Dynamics,* 2004.

[87] STANDARD, I. **Iso/iec/ ieee29119-2.** 2013,2013.

[88] SUBIC, N.; KRUNIÓ, T.; GEMOVIC, B. **Responsive web design - are we ready for the new age?** *Online Journal of Applied Knowledge Management,* **2,** 2014.

[89] SUTCLIFFE, A.; HART, J. **Some reflections on evaluating users' experience.** *which is commonly known as TwinTide (Towards the Integration of Trans-sectorial IT Design,* p. 67, 2013.

[90] SYDIK, J. J. **Design accessible web sites.** *Thirty-Six Keys to Creating Content for All Audiences and Platforms The Pragmatic bookshelf,* 2007.

[91] SYSTEMS, **W. A systematic literature review on process model testing: Approaches, challenges, and research directions.**

[92] TOMLIN, C. **A Comprehensive Review and Matrix of 14 Usability Testing Tools.** Website, Accessed August 2015. Available at http://www.usefulusability.com/14- usability-testing-tools-matrix-and-comprehensive-reviews/.

[93] UFPA. **Chi-Square.** Website, Accessed in July 2015. Available at http://www.ufpa.br/dicas/biome/bioqui.htm.

[94] UFSCAR. **Laboratory of research on software engineering (lapes).** Website, Accessed in January 2015. Available at http://lapes.dc.ufscar.br/.

[95] UNGER, R.; CHANDLER, C. **A Project Guide to UX Design: For User Experience Designers in the Field or in the Making.** Voices That Matter, 2009.

[96] UNIVERSITY, 0. M. **CMMI (Capability Maturity Model Integration.**

[97] VAN DER AALST, L. **Software Testing As a Service (STaaS).** *Pacific Northwest Software Quality Conference,* 2010.

[98] VEENENDAAL, E. V. **Test Maturity Model Integration (TMMi). 2012.**

[99] W3C. **Todos@web: National web accessibility award.** Website, Accessed in July 2015. Available at http://premio.w3c.br/.

[100] WATSON, D.; WIESE, D.; VAIDYA, J.; TELLEGEN, A. **Thetwogeneral activation systems of affect: Structural findings, evolutionary considerations, and psychobiological evidence.** *Journal of personality and social psychology,* 76(5):820,1999.

[101] WHITTAKER, J. **Exploratory Software Testing.** 2009.

[102] WOOTTON, B. **Preparing for Continuous Delivery.**

[103] WORKSHOPS, V. **Organisation of testing activities in Norwegian Software Compa- nies**. 2013.

[104] WROBLEWSKI, L. **Multi-Device Layout Patterns.** Webpage, Accessed August 2015. Available at http://www.lukew.com/ff/entry.asp71514.

[105] WROBLEWSKI, L. **Mobile First.** A Book Apart, 2011.

[106] YANG, T.; BOLCHINI, D. **Branded interactions: Predicting perceived product traits and user image from interface consistency and visual guidance.** *Interacting with Computers,* p. iwt048, 2013.

[107] YESILADA, Y; BRAJNIK, G.; VIGO, M.; HARPER, S. **Understanding web accessibility and its drivers.** In: *Proceedings of the International cross-disciplinary conference on web accessibility,* p. 19. ACM, 2012.

[108] YESILADA, Y; BRAJNIK, G.; VIGO, M.; HARPER, S. **Exploring perceptions of web accessibility: a survey approach.** *Behaviour & Information Technology,* (ahead-of-print):1-16, 2013.

[109] YOUNGBLOOD, N. E.; YOUNGBLOOD, S. A. **User experience and accessibility: An analysis of county web portals.** *Journal of Usability Studies,* 9(1):25-41,2013.

APPENDIX A

Accessibility Test

A.l Category: Education

UF	Website	index	AccessMonitor Errors 1 Warnings		
			A	AA	AAA
AC	IFAC (www.ifac.edu.br)	5.0	14	6	4
AC	UFA (www.ufac.br)	3.6	19	5	5
AL	(IFAL) www2.ifal.edu.br	4.4	14	1	2
AL	(UFAL) www.ufal.edu.br	5.7	12	1	3
AM	(IFAM) www.ifam.edu.br	3.9	17	6	6
AM	(UFAM) www.ufam.edu.br	4.7	17	4	4
AP	(IFAM) www.ifap.edu.br	5.2	14	6	4
AP	(UNIFAP) www.unifap.br	3.7	14	1	1
BA	(IFBAIANO) www.ifbaiano.edu.br	4.2	15	4	2
BA	(IFBA) www.ifba.edu.br	4.1	18	3	5
BA	(UFBA) www.ufba.br	5.6	14	3	4
BA	(UFOB) www.ufob.edu.br	5.2	12	4	6

BA	(UFRB) www.ufrb.edu.br	6.3	12	4	6
BA	(UFSB) www.ufsb.edu.br	5.0	11	4	2
EC	(IFCE) www.ifce.edu.br	4.5	18	4	5
EC	(UNILAB) www.unilab.edu.br	5.0	16	5	5
EC	(UFCA) www.ufca.edu.br	6.5	10	3	3
EC	(UFCE) www.ufc.br	6.4	13	1	1
DF	(IFB) www.ifb.edu.br	4.9	11	3	4
DF	(UNB) www.unb.br	3.8	20	3	2
ES	(IFES) www.ifes.edu.br	4.7	15	2	3
ES	(UFES) www.ufes.br	4.4	15	4	3
GO	(IFGOIANO) www.ifgoiano.edu.br	4.7	15	3	3
GO	(IFG) www.ifg.edu.br	5.4	14	4	4
GO	(UFG) www.ufg.br	4.8	12	5	5
MA	(IFMA) www.ifma.edu.br	4.0	21	7	6
MA	(UFBA)www.ufba.br	3.6	15	2	4
MG	(CEFET/MG) www.cefetmg.br	5.6	14	2	2
MG	(IFMG) www.ifmg.edu.br	4.6	14	4	5
MG	(IFNMG) www.ifnmg.edu.br	4.5	15	4	4
MG	(IFSEMG) www.ifsudestemg.edu.br	5.4	14	2	2
MG	(IFSULDEMINAS) www.ifsuldeminas.edu.br	4.6	16	5	5
MG	(IFTM) www.iftm.edu.br	5.9	10	1	1
MG	(UNIFAL) www.unifal-mg.edu.br	4.0	16	5	4
MG	(UNIFEI) www.unifei.edu.br	4.2	18	4	3
MG	(UFJF) www.ufjf.br	4.3	16	3	5
MG	(UFLA) www.ufla.br	4.6	16	2	3
MG	(UFMG) www.ufmg.br	4.0	16	2	2
MG	(UFOP) www.ufop.br	4.2	15	3	4
MG	(UFSJ) www.ufsj.edu.br	2.9	17	3	4
MG	(UFU) www.ufu.br	5.3	12	2	3
MG	(UFV) www.ufv.br	3.8	5	2	0
MG	(UFVJM) www.ufvjm.edu.br	4.5	12	5	5
MG	(UFTM) www.uftm.edu.br	3.5	16	4	2
MG	(UFGD) www.ufgd.edu.br	3.5	13	5	1
MS	(IFMS) www.ifms.edu.br	4.6	15	2	3
MS	(UFMS) www.ufms.br	4.3	12	1	3
MT	(IFMT) www.ifmt.edu.br	4.2	16	1	3
MT	(UFMT) www.ufmt.br	3.7	15	1	3
PA	(IFPA) www.ifpa.edu.br	0	0	0	0
PA	(UFOP) www.ufop.br	5.0	15	4	4
PA	(UFPA) www.portal.ufpa.br	3.5	14	0	3
PA	(UNIFESSPA) www.unifesspa.edu.br	5.6	13	3	4
PA	(UFRA) www.portal.ufra.edu.br	4.3	17	6	7
PB	(IFPB) www.ifpb.edu.br	6.5	14	2	3
PB	(UFPB) www.ufpb.br	5.1	16	3	2
PB	(UFCG) www.ufcg.edu.br	3.5	17	5	2
PB	(UNIVASF) www.univasf.edu.br	3.3	16	2	1
PE	(IFPE) www.ifpe.edu.br	5.0			
PE	(IFSERTAO) www.ifsertao-pe.edu.br	4.3	16	5	3
PE	(UFPE) www.ufpe.br	3.9	16	3	2
PE	(UFRPE) www.ufrpe.br/br	3.4	17	1	2
PI	(IFPI) www5.ifpi.edu.br	3.4	18	4	2
PI	(UFPI) www.ufpi.br	3.9	18	3	2
PR	(IFPR) www.curitiba.ifpr.edu.br	6.0	11	3	4
PR	(UNILA) www.unila.edu.br	6.2	13	4	4
PR	(UFPR) www.ufpr.br	5.1	12	3	4

PR	(UTFPR) www.utfpr.edu.br	5.9	14	1	4
RJ	(CEFET/RJ) www.cefet-rj.br	5.2	9	2	3
RJ	(ENCE) www.ence.ibge.gov.br	0	0	0	0
RJ	(IFRJ) www.ifij.edu.br	3.9	17	6	3
RJ	(IFFLUMINENSE) www.iff.edu.br	5.0	17	2	4
RJ	(IME) www.ime.eb.br	5.6	13	3	4
RJ	(INES) www.ines.gov.br	4.2	14	4	3
RJ	(UNIRIO) www.unirio.br	6.5	12	0	3
RJ	(UFRJ) www.ufij.br	3.2	16	3	5
RJ	(UFF) www.uff.br	6.8	15	5	2
RJ	(UFRRJ) www.ufrrj.br	2.8	23	4	3
RN	(IFNR) www.ifm.edu.br	7.6	11	1	3
RN	(UFRN) www.ufm.br	3.5			
RN	(UFERSA) www2.ufersa.edu.br	5.0	13	3	5
RO	(UNIR) www.unir.br	4.1	14	3	2
RO	(IFRO) www.ifro.edu.br	3.6	15	3	3
RR	(IFRR) www.ifir.edu.br	4.9	15	4	5
RR	(UFRR) http://ufrr.br	4.8	15	4	5
RS	(UFCSPA) www.ufcspa.edu.br	5.0	16	2	2
RS	(UNIPAMPA) www.unipampa.edu.br	6.4	14	2	2
RS	(IFRS) www.ifrs.edu.br	5.9	14	2	3
RS	(IFFARROUPILHA) www.iffarroupilha.edu.br	5.4	17	1	3
RS	(IFSUL) www.ifsul.edu.br	4.8	21	2	2
RS	(UFPEL) www2.ufpel.edu.br	4.1	14	1	2
RS	(UFMS) www.ufms.br	5.8	10	5	5
RS	(FURG) www.furg.br	2.9	17	7	2
RS	(UFRGS) www.ufrgs.br	4.4	14	3	3
SC	(IFCATARINENSE) ifc.edu.br	4.8	14	1	5
SC	(IFSC) www.ifsc.edu.br	3.5	21	6	6
SC	(UFFS) www.uffs.edu.br	3.3	17	3	3
SC	(UFSC) http://ufsc.br	5.8	7	1	0
SE	(IFS) www.ifs.edu.br	5.7	18	5	2
SE	(UFS) www.ufs.br	4.7	14	3	2
SP	(UFABC) www.ufabc.edu.br	3.9	19	5	3
SP	(IFSP) www.ifsp.edu.br	4.7	17	5	4
SP	(ITA) www.ita.br	6.4	11	0	3
SP	(UFSCAR) www.ufscar.br	4.1	16	2	1
SP	(UNIFESP) www.unifesp.br	4.8	13	4	4
TO	(UFT) www.uft.edu.br	4.4	14	3	3
TO	(IFTO) www.ifto.edu.br	3.3	18	5	2

A.2 Category: e-Commerce

Website	index	AccessMonitor Errors 1 Warnings		
		A	AA	AAA
www.shopfato.com.br	6.3	13	3	0
www.americanas.com.br	5.1	11	5	2
www.fujioka.com.br	6.7	7	0	0
www.saraiva.com.br	4.3	16	4	4
www.mercadolivre.com.br	4.8	11	2	3
www.dafiti.com.br	3.8	17	5	3
www.magazineluiza.com.br	4.3	13	2	2
www.submarino.com.br	4.7	13	4	4
www.walmart.com.br	4.3	16	3	3

www.netshoes.com.br	4.7	13	2	5
ww.buscape.com.br	4.7	13	2	5
www.fastshop.com.br	6.1	7	1	0
www.ricardoeletro.com.br	5.5	6	1	0
www.colombo.com.br	3.5	16	5	3
www.marisa.com.br	3.3	17	4	3
www.tokstok.com.br	6.1	7	1	0
www.kalunga.com.br	5.5	6	1	0
www.onofre.com.br	3.3	20	3	1
www.voegol.com.br	4.1	16	2	2
www.drogariasantamarta.com.br	4.2	13	1	1
www.hipermoreira.com.br	3.5	13	2	3
www.dellapanificadora.com.br	3.1	17	4	1
www.centauro.com.br	3.2	20	6	5
www.natura.com.br	3.4	19	3	4
www.oboticario.com.br	3.6	18	1	4
www.loja.havaianas.com.br	4.7	14	2	0
www.alobebe.com.br	3.7	15	4	6
www.cobasi.com.br	3.4	18	4	4
www.myshopbrasil.com.br	5.9	13	1	3
www.cea.com.br	4.4	15	0	3
www.paodeacucar.com.br	3.2	19	4	4
www.decolar.com	3.5	16	3	3
www.amazon.com.br	3.9	16	5	5
www.hotelurbano.com.br	4.8	13	2	2
www.livrariacultura.com.br	3.3	18	4	4
www.loja.electrolux.com.br	3.8	14	1	3
www.bluetree.com.br	3.4	15	4	2
www.shop2gether.com.br	5.4	11	3	0
www.assine.abril.com.br	3.4	14	4	3
ipanema.loj agrendene.com.br	4.1	14	5	3
www.fundacaodorina.org.br	6.6	12	1	1
loja.bridgestone.com.br	4.0	18	2	3

A.3 Category: Entertainment

Website	index	AccessMonitor		
		Errors 1 Warnings		
		A	AA	AAA
www.legendasonora.com.br	6.5	10	4	4
www.midiace.com.br	6.1	10	0	2
www.youtube.com.br	6.0	10	1	3
www.msn.com.br	4.7	13	2	3
www.globo.com	4.3	15	0	3
www.r7.com	3.7	17	4	3
www.aliexpress.com.br	5.0	15	3	5
www.terra.com.br	6.9	7	1	3
www.maissentidos.org.br	8.0	9	2	3
www.ig.com.br	3.9	16	4	4
www.linkedin.com	6.3	10	1	2
www.netflix.com.br	4.3	14	0	2
www.uol.com.br	3.7	18	1	3
www.flickr.com.br	4.7	12	5	5
www.about.com.br	5.1	14	2	5
www.forbes.com.br	3.7	14	5	4

APPENDIX B

Informed Consent Form

You are being invited to take part in a research project as a volunteer. My name is **Tiago do Carmo Nogueira**, I am a student on the Master's Programme in Computer Science at the Federal University of Goiás.

This research is being carried out as part of a master's thesis in Computer Science. It aims to investigate the difficulties and similarities in the experience of blind and sighted users of new trends on the Web.

If you have any questions about the research, you can contact the researcher in charge, **Tiago do Carmo Nogueira** by e-mail: ti- ago.nogueira@bag.ifmt.edu.br. If you have any questions about your rights as a participant in this research, you can contact the **Research Ethics Committee of the Federal University of Goiás** on the following telephone numbers: **3521-1075** or **3521-1076.**

CONSENT TO THE PERSON'S PARTICIPATION AS A RESEARCH SUBJECT

I understand that the information and recordings are for research purposes only and that my name and image will not be used for any other purpose. I waive any rights to the recordings and understand that the recordings may be copied and used only for this research.

I understand that participation in this study is voluntary and I agree to immediately raise any concerns or discomfort during the tasks proposed by the research with the researcher(s) responsible.

Please sign below to indicate that you have read and understood the information on this form and that any questions you may have about the session have been answered.

____

Research Participant

APPENDIX C

Research Subject Identification Questionnaire

Total blindness (congenital)() Total blindness (acquired)() User (sighted)()

Personal Information

01. Full name?

02. Date of birth?

03. What is your gender?

Educational Information

04. What is your level of education? What year did you finish?

05. If 3rd degree, what was the name of the course? When did you start?

Professional Experience

06. What is your profession?

07. How long have you been in the profession?

() Less than 1 year.

() Between 1 and 2 years.

() Between 2 and 4 years.

() More than 4 years.

Computer Expertise

08. How long have you been using a computer?

() Less than 1 year.

() Between 1 and 2 years.

() Between 2 and 4 years.

() More than 4 years.

09. Where do you use a computer? (You can tick more than one option).

() Home.

() Labour

() School.

() Other?

10. On average, how many hours a week do you use the computer?

() Less than 2 hours.

() Between 2 and 5 hours

() Between 5 and 10 hours.

() More than 10 hours.

11. Have you ever been involved in a usability/accessibility project?

() Yes.

() No.

12. Have you ever taken part in a usability test? If so, what type of site did you access?

13. Which assistive tool do you usually use?

APPENDIX D

Affect Grid Questionnaire (UX)

Evaluation Identification						
Application:	THE SOI	()S02	()S03	()S04	()S05	()S06

Task 01
Mark with an **X** on a scale of 1 to 9 how you felt when carrying out this task?

	1	2	3	4	5	6	7	8	9
Displeasure-Pleasure	( )	( )	( )	( )	( )	( )	( )	( )	( )
Sleepy-Anxious	( )	( )	( )	( )	( )	( )	( )	( )	( )

Task 02
Mark with an **X** on a scale of 1 to 9 how you felt when carrying out this task?

	1	2	3	4	5	6	7	8	9
Displeasure-Pleasure	( )	( )	( )	( )	( )	( )	( )	( )	( )
Sleepy-Anxious	( )	( )	( )	( )	( )	( )	( )	( )	( )

Task 03
Mark with an **X** on a scale of 1 to 9 how you felt when carrying out this task?

	1	2	3	4	5	6	7	8	9
Displeasure-Pleasure	( )	( )	( )	( )	( )	( )	( )	( )	( )
Sleepy-Anxious	( )	( )	( )	( )	( )	( )	( )	( )	( )

Task 04
Mark with an **X** on a scale of 1 to 9 how you felt when carrying out this task?

	1	2	3	4	5	6	7	8	9
Displeasure-Pleasure	( )	( )	( )	( )	( )	( )	( )	( )	( )
Sleepy-Anxious	( )	( )	( )	( )	( )	( )	( )	( )	( )

Task 05
Mark with an **X** on a scale of 1 to 9 how you felt when carrying out this task?

	1	2	3	4	5	6	7	8	9
Displeasure-Pleasure	( )	( )	( )	( )	( )	( )	( )	( )	( )
Sleepy-Anxious	( )	( )	( )	( )	( )	( )	( )	( )	( )

Task 06
Mark with an **X** on a scale of 1 to 9 how you felt when carrying out this task?

	1	2	3	4	5	6	7	8	9
Displeasure-Pleasure	( )	( )	( )	( )	( )	( )	( )	( )	( )
Sleepy-Anxious	( )	( )	( )	( )	( )	( )	( )	( )	( )

APPENDIX E

PANAS Questionnaire (UX)

Evaluation Identification						
Application:	THE SOI	()S02	()S03	()S04	()S05	()S06

Please mark with an X the option that best expresses your feelings at the very moment you read the sentences. Be as honest as possible and remember that there is no right or wrong answer.	Very little or not at all	A little	Moderately	A lot	Excessively
01. I feel interested	( )	( )	( )	( )	( )
02. I feel irritated	( )	( )	( )	( )	( )
03. I feel distressed	( )	( )	( )	( )	( )
04. I feel in a "state of alert"	( )	( )	( )	( )	( )
05. I feel energised	( )	( )	( )	( )	( )
06. I feel embarrassed	( )	( )	( )	( )	( )
07. I feel upset	( )	( )	( )	( )	( )
08. I feel inspired	( )	( )	( )	( )	( )
09. I feel safe	( )	( )	( )	( )	( )
10. I feel nervous	( )	( )	( )	( )	( )
11. I feel guilty	( )	( )	( )	( )	( )
12. I feel determined	( )	( )	( )	( )	( )
13. I feel scared	( )	( )	( )	( )	( )
14. I feel attentive	( )	( )	( )	( )	( )
15. I feel hostile	( )	( )	( )	( )	( )
16. I feel tense	( )	( )	( )	( )	( )
17. I feel enthusiastic	( )	( )	( )	( )	( )
18. I feel dynamic	( )	( )	( )	( )	( )
19. I feel proud	( )	( )	( )	( )	( )
20. I feel frightened	( )	( )	( )	( )	( )

APPENDIX F

Usability Questionnaire

Evaluation Identification						
Application:	THE SOI	()S02	()S03	()S04	()S05	()S06

Understanding verification questions

1. What is the purpose of the site?

Utility, Satisfaction and Ease of Use

2. In general, how easy is the site to use?

() Very difficult

() Difficult

() More or less

() Easy

() Very easy

3. Was the effort demanded?

() Very low

() Low

() Medium

() High

() Very high

4. How do you think the information is organised?

() Very bad

() Bad

() Fair

() Good

() Very good

5. Was the information accessible?

() Strongly disagree

() Disagree

() Neither agree nor disagree

() I agree

() Totally agree

6. Was the amount of information sufficient?

() Not at all

() Not very

() More or less

() Very

() Extremely

7. How are the screens laid out?

( ) Very confusing

() Confused

() Neither confusing nor clear

() Of course

() Very clear

8. Naming links?

( ) Very confusing

() Confused

() Neither confusing nor clear

() Of course

() Very clear

9. Assimilation of information?

() Very difficult

() Difficult

() More or less

() Easy

() Very easy

10. Is it easy to remember where things are?

() Very difficult

() Difficult

() More or less

() Easy

() Very easy

Usability Attributes I

11. How satisfied are you with the time it takes to complete the tasks?

() Dissatisfied

() Not very satisfied

() Neither satisfied nor dissatisfied

() Satisfied

() Very satisfied

12. Overall, the test was?

() Monotonous

() A bit monotonous

() Neither monotonous nor interesting

() Interesting

() Very interesting

13. Do you think the sites are designed for first-time visitors?

() Strongly disagree

( ) Disagree

() Neither disagree nor agree

() I agree

() Totally agree 14. Shortcuts?

() Extremely sufficient

() Sufficient

() Neither sufficient nor insufficient

() Insufficient

() Extremely insufficient

15. Are navigation errors easy to fix?

() Strongly disagree

() Disagree

() Neither disagree nor agree

() I agree

() Totally agree

Usability Attributes II

16. Can you find the information you want?

() Easily

() With little difficulty

() With great difficulty

() I can't find it

17. At some point while browsing, did the site lose its identity, i.e. did you feel like you were on another site?

() No

() Yes

18. Did you have any difficulty reading the site's content? If yes, what difficulties did you encounter?

() No

() Yes

19. Did you have any difficulty identifying any element of the site? If yes, what difficulties did you encounter?

() No

() Yes

20. Do you identify with the language of the site?

()No

() Yes

21. Did you find it difficult to navigate the site? If so, what difficulties did you encounter?

() No

() Yes

22. Which of the tasks do you think was the easiest?

23. Which of the tasks did you find most difficult? Why?

24. Have you used any research tools? If yes, what is the name of the tool?

()No

() Yes

25. In your opinion, what are the main qualities of this site? (Positive aspects).

26. In your opinion, what are the main defects of this site? (Negative aspects).

AT THE END

1. In view of the test carried out, what do you think is the best website among those visited? Please explain.

2. And which website is the worst? Explain.

APPENDIX G

User Performance

G.1 Category: Education

Suj	Education											
	S01 (Responsive)						S02 (Non-Responsive)					
	Task 1	Task 2	Task 3	Task 4	Task 5	Task 6	Task 1	Task 2	Task 3	Task 4	Task 5	Task 6
01	00:21	03:39	02:53	03:31	04:32	24:25	00:35	01:52	00:31	01:50	02:08	00:25
02	00:12	02:05	01:34	02:08	02:41	00:56	00:45	02:07	04:44	02:51	01:34	02:07
03	01:09	10:22	04:03	02:53	03:42	00:23	00:50	05:00	05:08	01:24	01:53	00:27
04	00:58	02:31	01:40	02:06	02:16	01:01	03:06	01:40	01:05	01:01	01:28	03:39
05	00:43	03:58	06:12	01:51	02:10	05:04	01:10	06:41	03:29	01:10	00:41	00:25
06	02:12	00:47	05:30	01:51	01:51	01:38	02:51	01:10	02:13	01:23	01:35	01:11
07	01:10	05:07	09:22	07:45	04:21	01:25	00:57	04:11	02:06	02:48	01:18	05:07
08	00:07	04:12	03:23	05:33	02:47	01:06	01:17	01:41	02:07	05:16	00:53	02:53
09	01:54	01:29	01:16	09:00	04:51	02:00	01:42	05:16	02:42	04:08	01:00	06:39
10	00:09	02:48	03:04	00:54	01:05	00:23	00:06	01:21	01:13	02:11	01:20	01:04
12	00:15	02:48	02:19	03:43	05:43	00:24	00:04	00:34	02:06	01:00	00:15	01:47
13	00:19	01:19	01:22	00:38	00:42	00:37	00:09	01:24	00:44	04:08	00:11	00:20
14	00:06	01:09	01:50	01:37	00:14	00:15	00:04	00:22	01:03	00:43	00:16	00:33
15	00:06	02:22	03:11	00:24	00:09	02:11	00:03	00:39	00:30	00:19	00:19	01:55
16	00:12	02:00	03:37	05:26	00:30	00:12	00:03	01:35	00:22	00:32	01:52	01:21
17	00:55	00:31	01:21	01:01	00:20	00:19	00:19	00:43	02:45	00:54	00:19	00:14
18	00:21	02:06	02:02	01:54	00:16	00:46	00:11	00:35	00:39	00:56	01:54	00:23
19	00:06	00:50	00:31	00:29	03:08	00:17	00:26	00:23	00:52	02:00	00:22	00:46

G.2 Category: e-Commerce

Suj	e-Commerce											
	S03 (Responsive)						S04 (Non-Responsive)					
	Task 7	Task 8	Task 9	Task 10	Task 11	Task 12	Task 7	Task 8	Task 9	Task 10	Task 11	Task 12
01	05:43	04:54	02:20	00:29	05:37	04:53	00:22	06:34	00:15	02:00	01:05	00:19
02	04:08	05:28	01:36	01:45	06:14	00:28	01:17	02:22	01:28	01:54	01:07	00:18
03	15:14	04:45	00:27	09:37	05:02	02:16	00:17	08:16	00:09	03:24	01:41	00:09
04	02:06	03:26	05:53	07:23	01:28	02:47	03:09	01:44	01:08	00:59	02:20	00:14
05	00:57	11:42	01:32	00:56	20:18	03:50	00:45	04:47	00:16	04:12	03:21	00:17
06	01:05	04:25	01:04	03:32	02:22	03:12	01:28	02:13	00:53	04:40	02:22	00:18
07	04:37	10:34	00:55	06:42	08:57	06:24	00:45	02:22	01:35	06:44	03:18	00:20
08	00:34	01:58	01:33	00:40	01:18	03:45	00:20	00:48	00:16	02:16	00:45	00:19
09	05:11	08:06	08:40	07:12	09:36	04:15	05:50	06:20	01:35	03:12	09:41	02:15
10	00:09	00:33	00:06	00:36	00:31	00:21	00:06	00:19	00:07	00:44	00:11	00:12
12	00:15	00:37	00:06	01:41	00:36	00:23	00:09	00:18	00:09	01:24	00:38	00:10
13	00:09	00:18	00:07	00:54	00:19	00:14	00:08	00:34	00:12	01:04	00:09	00:02
14	00:17	00:18	00:18	00:05	00:26	00:26	00:09	00:15	00:10	00:23	00:14	00:04
15	00:08	00:24	00:08	00:03	00:07	00:17	00:04	00:09	00:05	00:14	00:16	00:07
16	00:09	00:19	00:07	04:05	00:29	00:23	00:26	00:18	00:11	01:45	00:07	00:02
17	00:12	00:23	00:06	00:48	00:30	00:21	00:06	00:13	00:09	00:23	00:13	00:01
18	00:17	00:17	00:10	00:07	00:30	00:11	00:14	00:09	00:15	00:39	00:11	00:04
19	00:08	00:21	00:06	00:07	00:23	00:21	00:05	00:05	01:54	00:01	00:06	00:06

Sample of participants: users 01 to 09 (blind); users 10 to 18 (sighted).

G.3 Category: Entertainment

Suj	Entertainment

	S05 (Responsive)						S06 (Not Responsive)					
	Task 13	Task 14	Task 15	Task 16	Task 17	Task 18	Task 13	Task 14	Task 15	Task 16	Task 17	Task 18
01	00:16	04:45	04:30	00:23	01:47	01:32	01:00	01:07	02:55	00:23	02:29	00:51
02	00:11	01:43	02:42	00:35	02:47	02:04	01:07	02:04	01:21	00:45	01:10	01:10
03	00:28	02:02	00:50	01:06	01:46	01:59	01:37	01:06	00:47	01:47	00:58	01:39
04	02:38	01:51	02:26	01:13	02:21	02:52	01:38	01:58	00:36	00:35	01:05	01:48
05	00:51	06:18	04:29	00:53	05:57	04:27	03:25	03:46	02:14	00:25	00:41	03:25
06	01:26	02:31	00:51	02:35	01:41	03:51	01:19	02:26	01:23	00:27	00:25	02:03
07	00:21	05:22	03:33	02:31	04:37	04:19	01:16	03:33	01:56	06:16	02:05	01:39
08	00:11	02:24	00:39	00:27	01:18	00:37	01:03	04:53	00:29	00:24	01:30	01:02
09	01:44	07:41	01:44	03:53	02:19	03:26	05:54	01:45	02:32	01:17	00:49	02:52
10	00:07	00:48	00:29	01:04	00:06	00:45	00:05	01:39	00:28	00:25	00:45	01:00
11	00:07	00:36	00:09	00:22	00:06	00:40	00:06	00:37	00:36	00:16	00:28	00:47
12	00:06	00:38	00:25	00:20	00:06	00:26	00:07	00:55	00:20	00:12	00:39	00:30
13	00:12	00:33	00:19	00:28	00:08	00:45	00:10	01:13	00:36	00:16	00:35	01:57
14	00:10	00:38	00:21	00:25	00:07	00:34	00:06	00:47	00:27	00:23	00:31	00:58
15	00:10	00:40	00:47	02:01	00:15	00:37	00:08	01:04	00:17	00:14	00:30	01:08
16	00:09	00:45	00:20	00:22	00:07	00:37	00:10	01:07	00:26	00:11	00:27	00:47
17	00:09	00:45	00:22	00:20	00:58	00:49	00:07	01:28	00:26	00:19	01:25	00:33
18	00:13	00:37	00:16	00:14	00:10	00:35	00:44	01:16	00:21	00:24	00:25	00:47

Sample of participants: users 01 to 09 (blind); users 10 to 18 (sighted).

MIX
Papier aus verantwortungsvollen Quellen
Paper from responsible sources
FSC® C105338

Printed by Books on Demand GmbH, Norderstedt / Germany